Visitors From Outer Space

31801

Visitors From Outer Space
by Roy Stemman

Aldus Books London

Series Coordinator: John Mason
Design Director: Günter Radtke
Picture Editor: Peter Cook
Editor: Sally Burningham
Copy Editor: Mitzi Bales
Research: Frances Vargo
General Consultant: Beppie Harrison

EDITORIAL CONSULTANTS:

COLIN WILSON
DR. CHRISTOPHER EVANS

**Frontispiece: has the world had visitors from space?
Above: a UFO seen in the sky over France in 1974.**

Visitors From Outer Space

We live on a small greenish-blue sphere turning in infinite space — but are we alone in that immensity? Persistent reports are made of mysterious objects that pass us, linger, and even land. Are such stories true? In trying to answer, this book gives a balanced look at the history of UFOs.

Contents

1

The Coming of the Saucers

High above Kentucky the plane climbed at top speed in an effort to close on an unidentified object in the sky. It had been spotted by many observers below, including the control tower operators at Godman Air Force Base. Three F-51 Mustang fighters had been diverted from a training exercise in an attempt to identify the mysterious craft. Captain Thomas Mantell, flying the leading plane, had outdistanced his wingmen when his first dramatic radio call came to the tower: "I see something above and ahead of me, and I'm still climbing." Mantell was asked to describe what he could see. "It looks metallic and is tremendous in

Most sightings of mysterious objects in the skies have been ambiguous—reports have been of strange lights moving in a way that seems unlikely, or swiftly flying disks that wheel impossibly through the sky. But a few people claim to have seen these objects in much greater detail, and to have photographed them as well. Right: a photograph by George Adamski. Taken in California in December 1952, it is an object he identifies positively as a "scout ship" observing Earth from Venus.

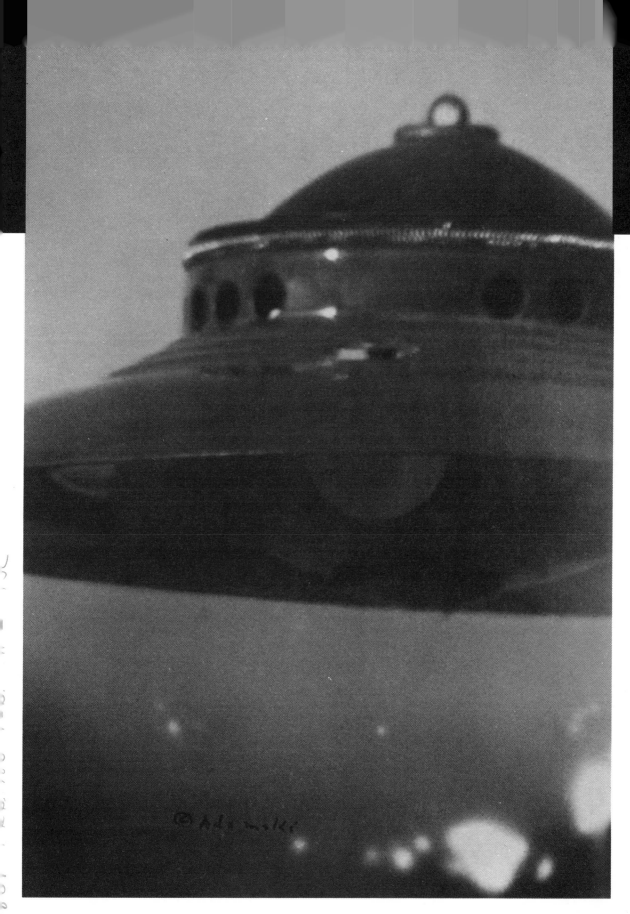

"Mantell's body was found near the remains of his aircraft..."

size . . ." Seconds later he called, "It's above me, and I'm gaining on it. I'm going to 20,000 feet." Those were the last words he spoke. Later on that fateful day of January 7, 1948, Mantell's body was found near the remains of his disintegrated aircraft, 90 miles from Godman Base. The unknown flying object had escaped. Some people believed that Mantell and his plane had been attacked by an alien spaceship, and rumors even spread that the dead pilot's body had been burned by a mysterious ray. The United States Air Force explanation did little to soothe growing public uneasiness about flying saucers. According to the USAF, the skilled veteran pilot, known to be level-headed and careful, had gone to his death chasing the planet Venus. It seemed incredible to most people that the experienced Mantell and the trained control tower observers could mistake a familiar heavenly body for an object described by some witnesses as "a huge ice cream cone topped with red."

Fifteen days after Mantell's death the USAF's official investigation of flying saucers—now more commonly referred to as UFOs or unidentified flying objects—went into operation. It was code named Project Sign, and its existence indicated that the authorities were in reality concerned about the strange aerial intruders which had flown into the headlines a little over six months before the Mantell incident.

On June 24, 1947, Kenneth Arnold saw nine shining disks weaving their way in formation among the peaks of the Cascade mountains of Washington state, and first alerted the world to the possibility that planet Earth was being visited by beings from another civilization. Arnold—a private pilot, member of the Idaho Search and Rescue Mercy Flyers, and Flying Deputy for the Ada County Aerial Posse—at the time was searching for a commercial plane that had crashed in the mountains. He was after a $5000 reward for locating the lost plane. Arnold never found the wreckage, but his sighting made him world famous.

Describing the flying objects he had seen to reporters, Arnold said that they moved "like a saucer skipping across water." An inventive reporter coined the phrase "flying saucer," and it soon became a household term—even flying into the pages of the dictionary. The popular term is not used by serious investigators, however. They prefer the more exact term UFO.

Kenneth Arnold was not the first man to see strange flying objects in the sky, nor even the first to describe them as saucer-like. A Texas farmer once saw a fast moving object in the sky and said that the only way he could describe it was as a large saucer. That was on January 24, 1878! Strange aircraft were also reported throughout World War II, and were often thought to be secret weapons of the enemy. But Arnold's sighting seemed to mark a turning point in UFO activity as well as supplying the media with a neat and colorful description. Perhaps it was because people recovering from a second major global war in only 25 years were hoping that there were wiser creatures in the Universe who could help put the Earth's troubles into perspective. Perhaps it was Arnold's estimate of the flying saucers' amazing speed of an incredible 1700 miles per hour that caught the public imagination. It might even simply have been the description of the flying crafts' shape that interested and amused people.

Left: Kenneth Arnold, a business man from Boise, Idaho. He made the first widely publicized sighting of unidentified flying objects in June 1947. The term "flying saucer" was coined by a reporter when Arnold said that the movement of the objects reminded him of how a saucer would look if skimmed across water.

Four days after Arnold's saucer sighting two pilots and two intelligence officers saw a bright light performing "impossible maneuvers" over Maxwell Air Force Base in Montgomery, Alabama. On the same day an Air Force jet pilot saw a formation of five or six unconventional aircraft near Lake Meade, Nevada. Another formation of flying saucers was seen by the pilot and copilot of a commercial DC-3 on July 4. They watched the five objects silhouetted against the sunset for 45 minutes. Soon after this group disappeared, a second formation of four came into view. Could they have been the same nine disks Arnold had seen? Only a few days later in early July a supersecret Air Force test center in the Mojave desert of California was being treated to a whole series of aerial visitations. The first sighting was by a test pilot at Muroc, now Edwards, Air Base. He was preparing for a flight in an experimental aircraft when he saw a yellow spherical craft moving against the wind. Several other officers at the base had seen three similar UFOs ten minutes earlier. Two hours later technicians at nearby Rogers Dry Lake saw a round object of aluminum appearance. After watching it for 90 seconds they decided that the strange craft was "man-made." Later that same day, a jet pilot flying 40 miles south of Edwards saw above him a flat object that reflected light. He tried to investigate but his aircraft could not climb as high as the UFO.

In the early days of UFO reports many people believed that Arnold and others had observed a new secret aircraft or guided missile being developed by the United States military. Arnold himself believed that for a time. But following a spate of sightings from reliable and competent witnesses—many of them experienced pilots fully aware of the latest aeronautical developments—the Air Force got jittery about UFOs. Behind the scenes the USAF was exploring the possibility that they belonged to a foreign power. After all, at the end of the war the Allies had obtained complete data on the latest German aircraft and missiles that had been under development. Had the Soviet Union uncovered a new aerodynamic concept from the German data? Or had they developed their own unique form of aircraft with which to spy on the United States?

It was soon clear that the Soviet Union could not have produced an aircraft that matched the flight characteristics of the UFOs in such a short period. Even if they had been able to do so, it was extremely unlikely that the Soviets would risk exposing the secret so soon by flying over so many countries. For, ever since Arnold had reported flying saucers skimming around the snow-clad mountain peak of Mount Rainier, UFOs had made appearances over every country in the world.

Once it was apparent that no nation on earth was capable of producing the UFOs, the possibility that another civilization was watching our planet had to be faced. This idea had already been

In the summer of 1947, shortly after Arnold's original sighting, UFO reports flowed in from all over the country as people scanned the sky eagerly and apprehensively. Above left: United Airlines pilot E. J. Smith saw a formation of five UFOs during a trip on July 4, 1947. His copilot verified the sighting. Smith is explaining that the plate he holds shows the approximate size of the disks as they looked to him from the plane.

Right: this photograph shows two of the three luminous objects that flashed across the skies of Kentucky in July 1947. Many observers of the glowing lights phoned the Louisville Weather Bureau with reports, and most described them as flying disks or saucers.

Above: Frank Ryman, a Coast Guard member, managed to photograph the "flying disk" he sighted near Seattle, Washington on July 4, 1947. He said it was white. Left: Ryman's photo enlarged 20 times, with the UFO indicated by an arrow. This was the very first photograph of a UFO. The Air Force claimed it was clearly a picture of a weather balloon.

Above: a movie camera being fitted into an F-51 fighter plane of the kind piloted by Air Force Captain Thomas Mantell at the time he was mysteriously killed chasing an unidentified flying object. The cameras were installed about six months after Mantell's death to enable pilots to photograph any strange objects they might encounter during flight.

Above right: a photograph of a skyhook balloon taken through a refracting telescope. At the time of Mantell's death, information on these secret balloons, designed to collect information from the fringes of the atmosphere, was highly classified. Mantell and the other pilots would not have known anything about these balloons. Official investigators claimed that such a balloon was what Mantell chased to his death.

put forward by some writers. But there was an alternative. Perhaps "saucer fever" had gripped the nation, causing ordinarily cautious people—and even experienced observers—to see UFOs in everyday objects. This seemed to be the official line as report after sensational report was explained away as balloons, birds, meteorites, planets, conventional aircraft, or natural phenomena. So why did investigations under Project Sign continue, to be followed in time by Project Grudge and Project Blue Book? Because a small but significant percentage of UFOs reported remained unidentified and unexplained as natural phenomena after experts had ruled out every known possibility. Often these were the best reports in the files in terms of the reliability of witnesses or the standard of supporting evidence such as radar reports.

The military establishment worried that a foreign power could use the flying saucer craze as a cover for spying over United

States territory, because the deluge of UFO reports that accumulated during the late 1940s caused an understandable public apathy about objects in the sky. Not that people were no longer concerned, but in most cases it had become physically impossible to do more than log in reports in the hope that some pattern would emerge from the data to aid ultimate identification. Yet until the origin of UFOs was known, they had to be regarded as a potential threat.

After six months of intensive saucer activity, even the most nervous citizens had to admit that if the saucers were hostile they were taking a long time to show it. Then, after the devastating news of Captain Mantell's death, public disquiet increased. At the official level, Project Sign investigators learned that same year of a pilot's duel with a flying saucer. It happened near Fargo, North Dakota on October 1, 1948. Lieutenant George F. Gorman of the North Dakota Air National Guard, was nearing the air base after a cross-country flight. When he had radioed for landing instructions, the control tower had told him that a Piper Cub was the only other aircraft in the vicinity, and Gorman could see the light aircraft below him as he made his approach. Suddenly a light passed him to the right. He thought it was the tailplane light of another aircraft, and called the control tower to complain. When he was told there was nothing else in the sky except the Piper Cub he decided to pursue the light.

As he turned to intercept he could see the other aircraft clearly silhouetted against the city lights. The mysterious light, however, did not appear to be attached to a solid body. Gorman closed in at maximum speed. At 1000 yards he could see that the light was six to eight inches in diameter and blinking. When he got this close, the light became steady and the aircraft banked sharply to the left with his jet on its tail. After a series of abrupt maneuvers Gorman found himself on a collision course with the UFO. When it became clear that the light was not going to take evasive action the National Guard pilot took a dive. The saucer missed the plane's canopy with only feet to spare. The "duel of death" continued, and Gorman had to dive a second time to avoid a head-on collision. Moments later the strange light began to climb. It disappeared as a shaken Gorman returned to Fargo to file his astonishing report.

His account to the Air Technical Intelligence Center (ATIC) included these words: "I had the distinct impression that its maneuvers were controlled by thought or reason." Four other observers saw a fast moving light in Fargo at the same time, but no one witnessed the dogfight.

To saucer advocates, the Mantell and Gorman cases were sufficient proof that superior beings in vehicles of advanced technology were patrolling our skies. Some assumed they were hostile, or at least capable of retaliating if pursued. Others thought the Mantell incident was an accident, and that the Gorman case was no more than a playful game on the part of the spacemen. Meanwhile the Air Force maintained the line of dismissing reports publicly while investigating them with renewed intensity. Their reasoning became clearer with the publication of the late Captain Edward J. Ruppelt's book *The Report on Unidentified Flying Objects*, published in 1956. Ruppelt had been

The UFO that Killed

At 1:15 p.m. on January 7, 1948 the control tower of Godman Air Force Base in Kentucky got a phone call from the State Highway Patrol. They said that townspeople about 80 miles away had reported seeing a strange aircraft in the sky. Godman personnel checked and informed the police that there were no flights in the area. Not long afterward, however, the control tower saw the object, which no one could identify.

About an hour later, three F-51 Mustang fighters on a training exercise came into view. The Base commander asked Captain Thomas Mantell, the leader, to investigate the unknown flying object.

All the Mustang pilots knew that to go beyond 15,000 feet without oxygen was dangerous. Yet at 2:45 p.m. Mantell told the control tower that he was going to climb higher to get closer to the odd craft. When the others reached 15,000 feet, they could not contact Mantell, who was above them.

At 3 p.m. the control tower lost sight of the weird aircraft. A few minutes after that Mantell's plane dived, exploding in midair. The wreckage was found 90 miles away. The official explanation of Mantell's death was that he had been chasing Venus. Few believed this implausible reason—and the mystery remains.

**Above: Dr. Charles Moore, a
meteorologist. He observed a
UFO with four Navy enlisted men
as the group was busy launching
and tracking a weather balloon
as part of the preparation
for a skyhook balloon launch.**

chief of the USAF's Project Blue Book, successor to Project
Sign, from 1951 to 1953. Ruppelt tried to throw new light on
some of the famous early accounts that had remained unsatis-
factorily explained.

The Mantell case had nothing to do with the planet Venus, he
admitted. Ruppelt had discovered that Venus could not have
been visible at the time of the chase, though if it were it would
have been in the same place in the sky as the UFO. Ruppelt
offered a far more plausible explanation. Mantell died while
trying to intercept a secret skyhook balloon, he said. The skyhook
project, designed to collect information from the fringes of the
atmosphere by balloon, was highly classified when Mantell tried
to identify the UFO. Ruppelt claimed that everyone involved in
the official investigation of the Mantell case was convinced that
he had been after a spaceship, so no one bothered to "buck the
red tape of security to get data on skyhook flights." By the time
Ruppelt checked on this possibility there were no longer any
records of the 1948 skyhook flights, but those involved thought
that at that time they were being launched from Clinton County
Air Force Base in southern Ohio. Winds records for the day in
question showed that a skyhook launched from Clinton would
have been visible from all the points in the area of Godman Base
from which the UFO was seen. The skyhook would have
climbed to 60,000 feet, and then drifted in a southerly direction.
Mantell died because he did not know he was chasing a balloon,
Ruppelt argued. "He had never heard of a huge 100-foot
diameter balloon, let alone seen one," he explained. If a skyhook
balloon had been launched from Clinton on January 7, even the
staunchest believers in flying saucers would have to admit that
the facts and description of the sightings tally beyond doubt.
If, however, it could be proved that no skyhook balloons climbed
into the jet stream over the Godman area that day, then even the
saucer skeptics would have to admit that the object which took
Captain Thomas Mantell to his death remains one of the most
perplexing puzzles of the UFO enigma.

Ruppelt offered an equally plausible explanation for Gorman's
strange duel with a flying saucer. Gorman was fighting a small
lighted balloon, he said in his book. An almost identical incident
had occurred over Cuba in September 1952. A Navy pilot, who
spotted a large orange light to the east after making practice
passes for night fighters, was told that no other aircraft were in
the vicinity. He tried to intercept the flying object. At closer
quarters he described it as having a green tail between five and
10 times its diameter. It seemed to be climbing, changing course,
and even responding to his plane's movements. After reaching
35,000 feet, the light began a rapid descent. The pilot took two
runs at it on a 90-degree collision course. On both occasions the
object traveled across his bow. On the third run he reported that
he came so close to the light that it blanked out the airfield below
him. Then it dived, and although the pilot followed, he lost the
light at 1500 feet.

"In *this* incident," Ruppelt wrote, "the UFO *was* a balloon."
This was proved by sending a lighted balloon up the following
night and ordering the pilot to compare his experiences. "He
duplicated his dogfight—illusions and all . . . Gorman fought a

Above: a picture of a skyhook balloon being inflated, one of a group released by the Navy in an attempt to explain the rash of UFOs. Right: a skyhook balloon in flight. The balloons were 100 feet long, and moved at up to 200 miles per hour when swept along by winds. Below: a flying saucer reported over London. This UFO turned out to be a high-level cosmic radiation balloon released by a university.

lighted balloon too. An analysis of the sighting by the Air Weather Service sent to ATIC in a letter dated January 24, 1949, proved it."

Did it? Major Donald E. Keyhoe, a staunch advocate of the interplanetary spaceships theory and a well-known author of UFO books, agrees that a weather balloon was released in Fargo on the night of Gorman's strange encounter. But he maintains that the Weather Bureau observer who tracked it recorded a course that took it away from the area in which the aerial duel was fought.

Even if the Mantell and Gorman cases were misidentification of different types of balloons, the fact remains that the U.S. Air Force had many more startling cases in its files about which the public knew nothing. An ATIC study of the flying saucer reports received in the year after the Kenneth Arnold sighting had culminated in an historic, top secret "estimate of the situation," which concluded that UFOs were interplanetary. Air Force Chief of Staff General Hoyt S. Vandenberg was not convinced, however, and rejected the report.

Whether people believed in them or not made no difference to the flying saucers. They continued to appear with startling regularity, often giving ground observers spectacular displays of aerial acrobatics.

As officialdom found new explanations for the UFOs, they appeared to be proving their own theories wrong. Mantell, for example, may have died while chasing a skyhook, but it was certainly not possible to dismiss all unidentified flying objects as huge metallic-looking balloons. On one occasion near the top secret White Sands Proving Grounds in New Mexico, the crew of an aircraft was tracking a skyhook when they saw two disks fly in from just above the horizon, circle the balloon at nearly 90,000 feet, and rapidly depart. When the balloon was recovered it was ripped. Captain Ruppelt, who published this account, does not specify the date but it would have been in either 1948 or 1949. Compare it with the experience of six observers in 1951. Two of the witnesses were from General Mills, whose aeronautical division had launched and tracked every skyhook balloon prior to mid-1952. The other witnesses were from Artesia, New Mexico. The group had been watching the movements of a skyhook for about an hour when one of them noticed two specks on the horizon. He pointed them out because two aircraft were expected at Artesia airport at about that time. But the specks were not aircraft. They flew in fast in close formation, heading straight for the balloon. They circled the skyhook once and flew off in the direction from which they had come, disappearing rapidly over the horizon. As they circled the skyhook the two dull white objects tipped on edge, and the observers saw that they had a disk shape. Their estimated size was 60 feet in diameter.

People who believed that UFOs were natural phenomena, such as meteorites, were finding it difficult to convince others because eminent astronomers and scientists were among the UFO observers. For example, the man who reported a flight of six or eight greenish lights in Las Cruces, New Mexico in August 1949 was Professor Clyde W. Tombaugh, discoverer of the planet Pluto. New Mexico was being plagued by a special type of UFO

Below: Dr. Lincoln La Paz, an authority on meteorites. When head of the University of New Mexico's Institute of Meteoritics, he became involved in the odd rash of reports of green fireballs in the skies of New Mexico in 1948 and 1949. Originally called in to help discover what the fireballs were, Dr. La Paz later sighted a fireball himself. He was certain it was not a meteor.

known as green fireballs. Dr. Lincoln La Paz, world-famous authority on meteorites, and a team of intelligence officers made a full investigation of the sightings. Many of them saw the green fireballs—including La Paz—but no physical evidence was found to show that they were a special type of meteorite. In fact, Dr. La Paz concluded that whatever they were, they most certainly were not meteorites.

Physical evidence was what was missing from all the early UFO reports, however good. There were many excellent visual reports, but no photographs or film of sufficient quality to aid identification. There were intriguing radar reports of strange fast-moving objects. But without visual corroboration that an object was where the radarscope recorded it, the report had to be dismissed as either a malfunction of the equipment or a misidentification of an echo caused by weather, birds, or other familiar objects. What the saucer buffs needed to prove their case was a sighting that combined visual and radar evidence. Gradually such reports began to trickle through, building up to a flood, with an astonishing visitation in the skies to the Capital itself.

The spectacular began in the dying hours of July 19, 1952, when two radars picked up eight unidentified objects on their screens at Washington National Airport. Whatever the objects were, they were roaming the Washington area at speeds of between 100 and 130 miles per hour. They would suddenly accelerate to "fantastically high speeds," and leave the area. The long-range radar in Washington has a 100-mile radius, and was used for controlling all aircraft approaching the airport. The National Airport's control tower was equipped with a shorter range radar designed for handling planes in its immediate vicinity. Just east of the airport was Bolling Air Force Base, and ten miles further east was Andrews Air Force Base, which were also equipped with short-range radar. All these airfields were linked by an intercom system. All three radars picked up the same unknown targets. One object was logged at 7000 miles per hour as it streaked across the screens, and it was not long before

Above: a drawing of the fireball seen by Dr. La Paz and his wife. It is based on the original drawing done by Mrs. La Paz. Dr. La Paz said that the fireballs were too big, their trajectory too flat, and their color too green for them to be ordinary meteors. Below: Dr. Clyde Tombaugh, the discoverer of the planet Pluto. He also saw the mysterious green lights in Las Cruces, New Mexico.

Above: an artist's melodramatic impression of the "Washington Flap" of July 19, 1952. On that night airport radars picked up a formation of UFOs flying over the White House and the Capitol. Below: a group of glowing objects in the sky over Salem, Massachusetts taken by a Coast Guard photographer on July 16, 1952. It was released by the Coast Guard at the height of the UFO craze.

the UFOs were over the White House and the Capitol, both prohibited flying areas. Radar experts were called in to check the equipment, though it was clear that the odds against three radarscopes developing identical faults were exceptionally high. They were found to be in good working order. Visual sightings were made as airline pilots came into the area and saw lights they could not identify. The lights were exactly where the radars were picking up UFOs. A commercial airline pilot was talking to the control tower when he saw one of the lights. "There's one—off to the right—and there it goes," he said. As he reported, the controller had been watching the long-range radar. A UFO that had shown to the airliner's right disappeared from the scope at the very moment the pilot said it had.

One of the best ground sightings that night came when the long-range radar operator at the airport informed Andrews Air Force Base tower that a UFO was just south of them, directly over the Andrews radio station. When the tower operators looked out they saw a "huge fiery orange sphere" hovering in the sky at exactly that position.

Incredible as it may seem, no one thought to inform ATIC. and it was nearly daylight when a jet interceptor arrived over the area to investigate the phenomena. Its crew searched the skies, found nothing unusual, and left—but the UFOs had left the radar screens by then in any case.

A week later almost to the hour, the flying saucers were back over Washington to give a repeat performance. The same radar operators picked up several slow-moving targets at about 10:30 p.m. on July 26. The long-range radar operators began plotting them immediately. They alerted the control tower and Andrews Base, but it already had them on its screens and were plotting them. A call went out for jet interceptors. Once again there was a delay but two jets finally arrived soon after midnight. The UFOs mysteriously vanished from the screens just as the jets arrived. The pilots could see nothing during their search, and returned to base. Minutes after the jets left the Washington area the UFOs came back! The jets were called back, and this time when they reached the area, the UFOs remained. The controllers guided the pilots toward groups of targets, but each time the objects flew away at great speed before the pilots could see more than a strange light. At times it seemed that the lights were somehow monitoring the control tower conversations with the pilots, and responding before an aircraft had time to change course. On one occasion a light remained stationary as the jet pilot flew at it with full power. As he closed in the light suddenly disappeared, like a light being switched off. Both Washington sightings lasted several hours, and the second one gave some of the Air Force's top saucer experts an opportunity to rush to the airport, watch the radar screens, and listen to the pilots' accounts.

After growing pressure from the press and public the Air Force held a press conference—the largest and longest since World War II. It was presided over by Major General John Samford, Director of Intelligence at the Pentagon. He offered no concrete explanation, but hinted that the lights came from strong temperature inversions, during which light waves are refracted or bent. Therefore an object on the ground or the moon, sun,

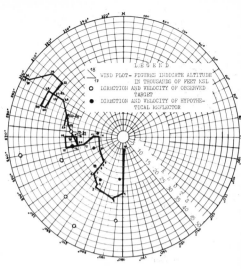

Above: an official Air Force diagram showing the position and course of the UFOs tracked over National Airport, Washington, D.C. during the night of July 26, 1952, a week after the first UFO sightings over the capital. Below: a physicist shows how an illuminated object can be formed naturally by temperature inversion. This was the official explanation of the Washington UFOs.

Above: Harry Barnes, the chief of radar at Washington's CAA control center where the mysterious blips were tracked, working over the radarscope that picked up the strange and unaccounted-for objects.

or stars may be reflected on a layer of inverted air. Similarly, temperature inversions could cause activity on radar screens.

However, the men controlling thousands of lives in and out of Washington National Airport had had years of experience, and were used to seeing and identifying every type of radar blip. They knew about temperature inversions, and were certain that they were not responsible for the radar UFOs whose blips came from solid objects. Besides, as Captain Ruppelt admitted much later, the temperature inversions known to exist on the nights in question were not strong enough to affect radar in the way they normally do. In fact, mild inversions existed on practically every night of June, July, and August 1952. The sensational Washington sightings therefore remain unexplained.

The 1950s progressed without any significant lull in flying saucer sightings. More good sightings were added to the bulging files, but none proved sufficiently outstanding to convince officialdom that the saucers were interplanetary. The public was easier to convince, and the ranks of the believers in UFOs grew all the time. Many asked what it would take to convince the authorities. The answer seemed to be nothing short of a mass landing on the White House lawn.

In August 1953 the Air Defense Command radar station at

Flying saucers were not just seen in the United States. UFO reports came from all around the world. Above: a "saucer nest" found in Queensland, Australia. A farmer claimed he had seen a spaceship that rose up out of a swamp. When he investigated, he found this "nest" with the reeds all flattened in a clockwise direction. Right: a British saucer society staring hopefully up at the sky. Below right: a possible saucer landing site? The president of the Norwegian UFO center bends over one of the several mysterious radioactive triangular impressions found in the Nams Fjord in 1972. Below: an artist's impression of a UFO that hurtled toward a DC-3 flying over Sweden. It finally shot underneath the plane.

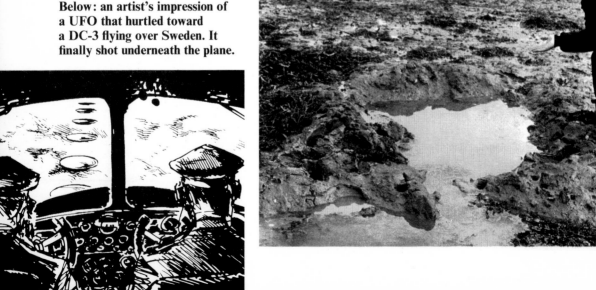

Ellsworth Air Force Base near Rapid City, South Dakota, picked up a "well-defined, solid and bright" target at the spot where a ground observer had reported seeing a light. Height-finding radar also recorded it at 16,000 feet. The object was almost stationary. Then it picked up speed, circled Rapid City, and returned to its original place in the sky. This maneuver was watched on radar and reported by the ground observer.

A jet hurried to the scene, and soon spotted the light. It closed in to within three miles of the object. Then the light sped off with the jet on its tail. There was a limit to how close the UFO allowed the aircraft to come before pulling away, as though its power supply was automatically linked to a device measuring the distance of its pursuer. Captain Ruppelt reported what happened next in *The Report on Unidentified Flying Objects*:

"The chase continued on north—out of sight of the lights of Rapid City and the base—into some very black night.

"When the UFO and the F-84 got about 120 miles to the north, the pilot checked his fuel; he had to come back. And when I talked to him, he said he was damn glad that he was running out of fuel because being out over some mighty desolate country alone with a UFO can cause some worry.

"Both the UFO and the F-84 had gone off the scope, but in a few minutes the jet was back on, heading for home. Then 10 or 15 miles behind it was the UFO target also coming back."

The alert pilots of the jet interceptor squadron at the base had heard the conversation between the controller and pilot. Another jet with a veteran of World War II and Korea at the controls was standing at the ready. This pilot wanted to see a flying saucer for himself. Permission was given and he climbed into the sky, spotted the UFO, and closed in. Once again the object sped away, keeping a three-mile distance. The pilot switched on his radar-ranging gunsight which in seconds showed that there was something solid in front of him. At that point he got scared and broke off the interception. The UFO, on this occasion, did not follow him back to base. That encounter, according to Ruppelt, "is still the best UFO report in the Air Force files."

Washington National Airport was the scene of more UFO activity in July 1955 when a brilliant circular object with a tail four or five times its length flew into the airport, stopped and hovered. It oscillated before taking off at high speed, and was caught in the beam of a searchlight; but the searchlight suddenly went out. According to Brinsley le Poer Trench, a well-known British author of flying saucer books, "The UFO also caused the ceiling lights at the airport to go out, but these lit up again the moment the UFO left the airport."

When the first decade of flying saucer activity was over, the puzzle remained. There were photographs, radar reports, and thousands of sightings from experienced observers. But the experts were no nearer solving the flying saucer mystery than they were when Kenneth Arnold's sighting hit the world headlines. Then the Soviet Union launched the first man-made satellite on October 4, 1957.

Humankind was on the verge of exploring space—and sending our own UFOs to other worlds.

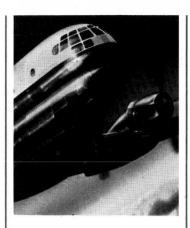

The UFO Escort

The Stratoliner of the British Overseas Airways Corporation (now British Airways) was three hours out of New York on its run to London. At that point, Captain James H. Howard and his copilot noticed some strange uninvited company three miles off their left side: a large elongated object and six smaller ones. These UFOs stayed along-side for about 80 miles.

As the plane neared Goose Bay, Canada for refueling, the large UFO seemed to change shape, and the smaller ones converged on it. Captain Howard told the Goose Bay control tower what was happening. Ground control in turn alerted the USAF, which sent a Sabre fighter to the scene. When Captain Howard contacted the Sabre pilot, he said he was coming from 20 miles away.

"At that," said Captain Howard, "the small objects seemed to enter the larger, and then the big one shrank." He didn't find out what finally occurred because he had to leave Goose Bay on schedule.

These events took place in June 1954. The pilot and co-pilot described the UFOs as spaceships, and were confirmed in this belief by various passengers. However, in a 1968 report by a USAF-sponsored research team, this close-range sighting was dismissed as an "optical mirage phenomenon."

The Conspiracy of Silence

Mass hysteria gripped the United States as thousands of citizens prepared for a Martian invasion. People fled madly from their homes and many of them reported seeing the invaders. This widespread panic, however, had nothing to do with flying saucers. It happened in 1938, nine years before flying saucers were reported, and it was caused by a radio dramatization by Orson Welles of H. G. Wells' science fiction story *War of the Worlds*. The broadcast opened as though it were a newscast. Thousands of Americans, tuning in late, believed they were listening to a real news flash—and did not wait to hear more.

The willingness to believe in invaders from beyond our world was shockingly demonstrated in 1938 when a dramatization of *War of the Worlds* created widespread panic among its radio audience. Above: Orson Welles, then an unknown, acted in the famous broadcast that he had also produced. Right: an illustration from the original magazine serialization of H. G. Wells' novel *War of the Worlds* in 1897. The artist has depicted the horrifying moment when the space creatures come out of their ominous machines.

"Was there a conscious decision for a cover–up?"

In the 1960s a similar reaction occurred in England when a TV drama included a mock news broadcast about a satellite that had been spotted in an orbit which kept it stationary over the British Isles. The make-believe news bulletin indicated that it might be armed with a nuclear weapon. People dashed out of their homes to warn others of the impending enemy attack before they realized they were watching a play rather than a news report.

If radio and television drama can cause such panic, what would be the reaction of the public to a government announcement that an alien race from another planet was watching us from the skies? UFO enthusiasts declare that it was fear of just such a panic that persuaded the United States government to hide the true facts about flying saucers from the American people. But was there a conscious decision for a cover-up among top-level personnel, or were they just as confused and puzzled as everyone else?

Flying saucer reports began to occur with regularity about two years after the end of World War II. People were still tense and jittery in the West from the effects of the War, and the strained relations with Communist countries added to everyone's feelings of unease. It was a period of diplomatic and military uncertainty, and in the United States especially the Air Force was nervous and jumpy about reports of strange objects appearing in the sky. They had the responsibility of discovering whether the UFOs were simply wild misidentifications of natural phenomena, enemy aircraft on spying missions, or visitors from outer space.

Alarmed by the possibilities of enemy spying or space visitations, the Air Force quickly set up its own investigation into unidentified flying objects under the wing of the Air Technical Intelligence Center (ATIC) as early as September 1947. This investigation, known by the various code names of Project Sign, Project Grudge, and Project Blue Book, lasted 22 years. It was finally wound up in December 1969. The United States was the only country to take the problem seriously enough to set up an investigation of this kind. It spent an immense amount of time and money over the years in trying to establish the facts. In many ways, partly through bad public relations and arbitrary changes in policy, the whole project backfired.

In the early days almost any object not readily identifiable by ground observers stood a chance of making headlines as a flying saucer in the local papers, and the Air Force was faced with numerous reports. But when all the reports had been sifted through, and those due to misidentification of known objects had been eliminated, there still remained a sizeable number for which there was no clear explanation. It was then that Air Force policy was at its weakest. While privately pursuing its own serious investigations into these sightings, it publicly derided the possibility of the existence of unidentified flying objects and attempted to fob off the press with feeble and unsatisfactory explanations. These explanations were just as unconvincing and contradictory to the public, which was generally more sophisticated and cynical than had been realized. It seemed too strange to many that trained pilots

Below: a 1946 U.S. Army test of a German V-2 rocket captured in World War II, carrying scientific instruments instead of explosives. It was known that the Soviets had also captured such rockets, and it was widely believed that they were testing them over U.S. territory. This gave rise to the fear that UFOs were the creation of the Cold War enemy in preparation for action against the United States.

Other captured German equipment
also fed fears of a Soviet attack.
Above: a German jet captured in
the Allied advance in 1945. The
GIs who found it abandoned, with
bombs ready for loading, reported
it "has no propeller and its
nose is shaped like a shark's."

Right: the Focke-Wulf Tiebflügel,
an upright, vertical takeoff
aircraft still in the design
stages at the end of the war.
At the end of each of the three
long arms of this technologically
advanced craft was a small jet
propulsion unit. The rotating arms
lifted the device from the ground
like the blades of a helicopter.

would suddenly start mistaking flocks of birds or reflections from their own planes as flying saucers when they never had done so before.

In 1950, in the face of Air Force denials that flying saucers existed at all, 94 percent of people interviewed in a nationwide poll in the United States said they believed in unidentified flying objects. Whether they thought that the Air Force was hiding the truth or was just too stupid to recognize it is not entirely clear. But one thing was certain—there was a yawning credibility gap between what the authorities told the public and what the public believed.

Edward J. Ruppelt, leader of Project Blue Book for two years, tried to establish what actually happened in the first years of the flying saucers. In his book *The Report on Unidentified Flying Objects*, he maintained that the conflicting statements issued to the press and the air of confusion were the genuine results of bewilderment and lack of coordination among Air Force staff. He didn't think the military was deliberately hiding the facts behind a smokescreen, as some critics later believed, but he admitted that if the Air Force had "tried to throw up a screen of confusion, they couldn't have done a better job."

Before setting up Project Sign in September 1947, the Air Technical Intelligence Center had made a preliminary study of flying saucer sightings, and had come to the conclusion that unidentified flying objects were real phenomena. Project Sign was accordingly given a priority rating and security coverage. Having accepted that flying saucers were real, the problem the

Above: the V-173, an experimental wingless aircraft known as the "flying pancake." This picture was released by the Navy in July 1947 during the first UFO excitement. The Navy said it was the only craft operated at that time which could answer the descriptions of the flying disks being sighted everywhere. But most of the sightings were in the far west, and this craft had never left Bridgeport, Connecticut.

Right: this official picture of the AVRO "disk" was released after the photograph above it hit the newspapers. A kind of hovercraft, the AVRO was jointly developed by the Air Force and Army. It never got more than four feet from the ground in tests, and was abandoned at the experimental stage.

top intelligence officers had to grapple with was their origin. After eliminating the possibility that they were a domestic secret weapon, possibly built by the Navy, there appeared to be two alternatives. Either they were some kind of spacecraft developed by the Soviet Union from Germany's leftover wartime designs, or they were interplanetary. All the German designs were carefully examined, but by the end of 1947 it was decided that there was no conceivable way in which the Soviet Union could have constructed a craft that behaved in the way unidentified flying objects did. The ATIC, still not questioning the assumption that UFOs were real, began to think that they must have come from outer space and that they had been built by a race with superior technological achievement. The problem that absorbed them was how to collect interplanetary intelligence. There were no appropriate guidelines or past experience for this task.

While these exciting ideas were being discussed in the Air Technical Intelligence Center, the Air Force continued to look foolish in its public stance. A statement put out from the Pentagon at about this time declared that flying saucers must

Right: in 1959 Jack Judges, a freelance cameraman, snapped a picture as he flew over the A.V. Roe Aviation Company's plant, and his lens caught this saucerlike aircraft sitting on the ground. The mystery craft was publicized as a possible secret weapon—one which might account for many of the flying saucer sightings of the previous 12 years.

Above: General Hoyt S. Vandenberg, Air Force Chief of Staff in 1948. He was supposed to have received a top secret report from Project Sign, the Air Force's own investigation into UFOs, later known by the code names Project Grudge and Project Blue Book. According to rumor, the Project Sign report was destroyed because it concluded that UFOs were interplanetary vehicles, and General Vandenberg refused to accept this conclusion for lack of proof.

Above right: the Lubbock Lights as photographed by a student at the Texas College of Technology. The phenomenon was seen on 14 occasions in 1951 in one of the best authenticated sightings of UFOs. Negatives of five shots of the Lubbock Lights were tested intensively and, according to the official statement, were "never proved to be a hoax, but neither were they proved to be genuine." Edward J. Ruppelt, former leader of Project Blue Book and author of an exposé of the investigation, said that such well-documented sightings were not taken into account enough by the Air Force.

be one of three things—reflections of the sun on low-hanging clouds, broken up meteors whose crystals had caught the rays of the sun, or large flattened hailstones that were gliding through the air. According to Ruppelt, a follow-up report was immediately issued which declared that these ideas were ridiculous. "No one had ever heard of crystallized meteors, or huge flat hailstones, and the solar reflection theory was absurd." No wonder the public was mystified and preferred to draw its own conclusions.

Why did the Air Force bother to issue ludicrous and unconvincing explanations that it was later obliged to retract? Was ATIC afraid of causing a panic if they voiced their real theories? Were they so unwilling to admit their own deep uncertainties that they took refuge behind an assortment of ill-considered excuses? Whatever the motives, the attitude of the Air Force with its claims and counterclaims, denials and false explanations, gave rise to a firm belief in a government conspiracy to cover up the truth about flying saucers. Arbitrary shifts in policy on flying saucers fanned this belief. After several years it had grown to such an extent that no serious attempt to study unidentified flying objects could be complete without an examination of the conspiracy claim.

It adds to the problem that most technologically advanced nations have secrets of some kind which they attempt to hide from other countries. Usually these secrets are known only to a few men. Even if the Air Force spokesmen who denied the existence of flying saucers believed what they said, the public could not be sure that these spokesmen—or even their superiors —had access to all the facts.

Many people at first believed the Air Force was pretending not to know about the strange flying disks because they were in

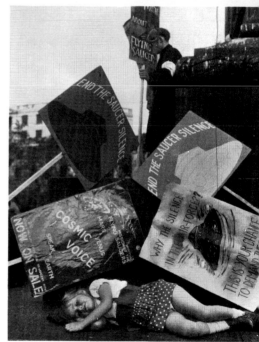

Above: E. J. Sullivan speaking to a meeting of the Civilian Saucer Investigations, one of the earliest nonmilitary organizations investigating UFO reports. Such groups were formed because of official skepticism about all flying saucers. Among CSI members was Dr. Walther Riedel (behind Sullivan), a renowned German rocket designer.

fact a new top secret weapon. But as the years passed and UFO reports came in from almost every country on the globe, it became apparent that this reason could not be applied to all governments.

In doubt that UFOs originated anywhere in the world, the public began to speculate on whether they originated in Outer Space. Air Force Intelligence meantime went through a series of shifts in attitude. On July 24, 1948 an incident that shook the staff of Project Sign took place. A large commercial plane nearly collided with a UFO, and the pilots were able to give an accurate description of it to ATIC investigators. No one at top level appeared interested, however.

Despite the fact that UFO sightings and reports kept getting better and better over the next months, it seemed that certain people in authority would not accept their reality under any circumstances. Gradually people working on Project Sign found that the Pentagon did not want information that might establish the existence of UFOs, but only explanations to prove that they didn't exist. This attitude was confirmed in February 1949 when the code name of Project Sign was changed to Project Grudge, and was staffed by those who would agree to follow the new policy of explaining each sighting in terms of misidentification or hallucination. But the press releases and articles approved by Project Grudge debunking flying saucers seemed to have the reverse effect on a public which knew that a lot of extremely reliable people, including air line pilots and

Above: pressure on officials to "end the saucer silence" was worldwide. Shown is a British UFO demonstration in London in 1958. The aim was to get the Royal Air Force to admit that the phenomenon of flying saucers existed. These enthusiasts were convinced that UFOs had an interplanetary origin.

scientists, had seen unidentified flying objects. The general suspicion that the Air Force was hiding the facts increased, and by December 1949 the public was ready for the sensational article written by Donald Keyhoe and published by *True* magazine.

The article was called "Flying Saucers are Real." The author maintained that after eight months of research he had reached the conclusion that the earth was being watched by intelligent beings from another planet, who traveled in vehicles that we called flying saucers. He examined some of the most puzzling saucer cases and demolished the Air Force's official explanations. His authoritative style, and the fact that *True* had a reputation for printing the facts, gave his story great impact. UFOs zoomed back into the headlines, and the article was picked up and discussed by TV and radio commentators all over the country. Keyhoe had played the security angle very strongly in his story. He had talked to certain top level contacts who had denied that UFOs were any kind of secret weapon. From this he had deduced that they must be interplanetary spaceships, and that the Air Force was covering this up. According to Ruppelt, who later looked into the question, the Air Force was not covering up. They had simply lost interest in the question of UFOs, and couldn't believe that anyone else was still concerned. However, the idea of a government conspiracy of silence took root even more strongly among many members of the public, especially those who had themselves investigated UFOs.

At the end of December 1949, despite a number of recent good sightings and the new public interest generated by the Keyhoe article, the Air Force decided to reduce operations in Project Grudge. It released a final report containing 600 pages of analyses and appendices. Despite the fact that 23 percent of the sightings mentioned fell into the "unknown" category, the report concluded firmly that UFO reports all originated from a mild form of mass hysteria.

To add to the general confusion, *True* magazine in March 1950 published another story that caused a furore. This time it was by the man in charge of a team of Navy scientists at White Sands, New Mexico. In an article entitled "How Scientists Tracked Flying Saucers" the author, Commander R. B. McLaughlin, described several UFO sightings made either by him or his crew at White Sands. About one of these he wrote: "I am convinced that it was a flying saucer, and further, that these disks are spaceships from another planet, operated by animate, intelligent beings." The story was surprising in itself. Even more startling, though, it had received complete military clearance despite the fact that it contradicted every military press release that had been issued over the last two years.

Who was the public to believe? When people like Commander McLaughlin risked their reputation by declaring a belief in the interplanetary origin of unidentified flying objects based on personal experience, it carried far more weight than the nonsensical explanations offered by faceless spokesmen for the Air Force. Part of the confusion was probably due to the fact

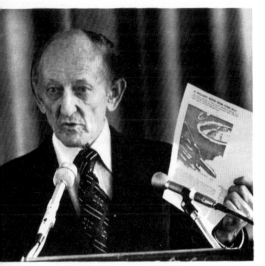

Above: Donald E. Keyhoe speaking on UFOs in 1973. A retired Marine Corps general, Keyhoe early maintained that UFOs are from outer space. His magazine article "Flying Saucers Are Real" caused a sensation in 1949.

Above: Dr. H. P. Robertson of the California Institute of Technology. He was the chairman of the CIA committee established in 1953 to investigate the UFO reports.

that even at the highest level one part of the Air Force seemed to have no idea what the other was doing about flying saucers. This became apparent in the investigation that followed the Fort Monmouth incidents.

In the summer of 1951 many radar reports of unidentified flying objects came in, and interest in the UFOs began to pick up among some of the staff at the Air Technical Intelligence Center. But since radar was known to do strange things under certain weather conditions, the reports did not attract official interest. All this changed starting September 10, 1951. At 11:10 a.m. on that day, at the Army Signal Corps radar center at Fort Monmouth, New Jersey, a student operator was trying to demonstrate automatic tracking on a radar set to an important group of visitors. The set was able to track objects flying at the speed of a jet. He saw an object about 12,000 yards southeast of the radar station, but was unable to locate it with the automatic tracking device. It was going too fast for a jet, he claimed. The weather conditions were checked but nothing was found that might have caused a faulty reading. Twenty-five minutes later a jet pilot flying over Point Pleasant, New Jersey saw far below him a silver disklike object, about 30 to 50 feet in diameter. At 3:15 p.m. that afternoon the radar at Fort Monmouth picked up an object traveling at the immense height of 93,000 feet. It could also be seen as a silver speck in

Above: Dr. Edward U. Condon, a physicist and head of the panel of scientists commissioned by the U.S. Air Force to investigate the flood of UFO reports in 1966.

Right: are UFOs really clouds? Odd formations like this one over Mount Rainier, Washington, were one of the suggestions by the Condon Committee as a natural explanation for saucer reports. The original Arnold sighting, incidentally, was made in this very area near Mount Rainier.

Below: a photograph of a UFO in flight over the Mount Palomar Observatory. It turned out to be simply a defect in the film.

the distance. Two more UFOs were picked up by radar the following day.

A copy of the report of the sightings was sent to Washington, and the Director of Intelligence of the Air Force ordered an immediate investigation.

This was followed by a top level conference at the Pentagon where it turned out that many of the generals and colonels present had no idea that the active work on UFOs had been largely curtailed. Orders were given to revitalize Project Grudge, and Captain Edward J. Ruppelt was put in charge. The project once more began to gain official prestige, and by March 1952 had become a separate organization known as the Aerial Phenomena Group. The discouraging name of Grudge was abandoned in favor of the code Blue Book.

Investigations into UFOs seem to have been conscientious and unbiased under Ruppelt, but the Press remained suspicious of a cover-up. After the extraordinary UFO sightings at Washington National Airport in July 1952, the Air Force had to call a press conference. It had the unfortunate result of again sounding like a cover-up.

One of the most disturbing—though perhaps not altogether surprising—elements of the flying saucer controversy is the revelation that the Central Intelligence Agency was involved in setting policy for UFO investigation in the first stages. In the early 1950s the CIA undertook a study of UFOs, aided by a panel of five scientists under the chairmanship of Professor H. P. Robertson of the California Institute of Technology. The Robertson Panel's report was completed in 1953. It was partially declassified in 1966. The report concluded that UFOs did not present a threat to national security, but it observed that "the continued reporting of these phenomena does, in these parlous times, result in a threat to the orderly functioning of the protective organs of the body politic."

What the panel feared was that channels of communication would become clogged with UFO reports. Even more serious, if an enemy could produce a UFO scare it might well be able to spring a surprise attack on the United States under cover of the flying saucers. The report went on to recommend a program that would "debunk" the UFOs, and educate the public in recognizing objects that might be mistaken for flying saucers.

There is no evidence that these recommendations were ever carried out. The Air Force continued to debunk saucers in public, but nothing was done to strip the subject of its aura of mystery. UFO reports continued to be filed by reliable and experienced witnesses and the number of sightings labeled "Unknown" grew to significant proportions.

What was needed was a completely impartial study of UFOs by independent scientists given access to Air Force files. UFO enthusiasts had demanded such an inquiry for years, and it came about as a result of a letter written by Major General E. B. LeBailly, then head of the Office of Information of the Secretary of the Air Force. It was dated September 28, 1965, and was addressed to the Military Director of the Air Force Scientific Advisory Board. After stating that 9265 UFO reports had been investigated by Project Blue Book between 1948 and

Left: a drawing of a proposed U.S. Air Force project in which an aircraft would eject and light gases to produce a huge bubble of burning gas, as shown. The project was designed to test how people would react if they saw this kind of bubble, which behaved and looked like many UFOs. The point was to see if people not only reported the bubble as a UFO, but also reported space visitors in connection with it. The test was never carried out.

Above: the Barra Da Tijuca UFO, which was sighted in May 1952, on the coast of Brazil near Rio de Janeiro. The two witnesses were a reporter and a photographer. This sighting, one of the better known ones, was shown up as a fraud by the Condon Committee investigators. They noticed that the shadow on the disk could only have been produced if the sun had been shining directly *up* from the surface of the water.

mid-1965, and that 663 of these could not be explained, he added:

"To date, the Air Force has found no evidence that any of the UFO reports reflect a threat to our national security. However, many of the reports that cannot be explained have come from intelligent and well qualified individuals whose integrity cannot be doubted. In addition the reports received officially by the Air Force include only a fraction of the spectacular reports which are publicized by many private UFO organizations.

"Accordingly, it is requested that a working scientific panel composed of both physical and social scientists be organized to review Project Blue Book—its resources, methods, and findings —and to advise the Air Force as to any improvements that should be made in the program to carry out the Air Force's assigned responsibility."

As a result an Ad Hoc Committee to Review Project Blue Book was set up. It recommended that the Air Force's UFO program should be strengthened "to provide opportunity for scientific investigation of selected sightings in more detail and depth than has been possible to date." After this, the University of Colorado agreed to undertake a study of UFOs under the direction of Dr. Edward U. Condon, a well-known physicist.

Here at last was the opportunity to find out what the UFOs were. The Colorado university study was to be an unbiased survey of the whole UFO scene conducted by experts in

Above: the Barra Da Tijuca UFO in the first of the five photographs obtained. This reportedly shows the UFO as it approached.

Left: another of the Barra Da Tijuca pictures. In this one the shadow on the disk in the air is on the right side of the UFO, whereas the shadows of the trees and shrubs on the ground appear to lie on the left side.

psychology, astronomy, radar, high-energy physics, meteorology, mathematics, astrophysics, aerophysics, chemistry, and many other relevant fields.

Most people who had distrusted the Air Force expected the truth from the Colorado project when it began its mammoth task of sifting the evidence on flying saucers in November 1966. But by the time its findings were released in January 1969, the belief that Dr. Condon and his fellow scientists were also party to a cover-up was widely held in flying saucer circles. Some civilian UFO organizations that initially enjoyed good relations with the Colorado project became dismayed by various events, and withdrew cooperation at an early stage. The official report seemed to justify their action. After more than two years of study the scientists concluded that what the

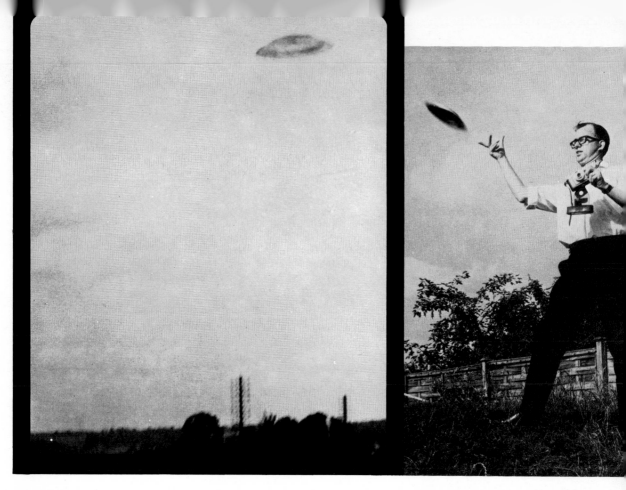

Air Force had maintained since the earliest flying saucer sightings was true: flying saucers did not exist.

The Colorado project ran into credibility problems in the first months of its existence. Dr. Condon addressed a meeting at which, according to the *Star-Gazette* of Elmira, New York, he said: "It is my inclination right now to recommend that the government get out of this business. My attitude right now is that there's nothing to it . . . but I'm not supposed to reach a conclusion for another year. Maybe it [the UFO riddle] would be a worthwhile study for those groups interested in meteorological phenomena." That statement was made less than three months after the project began, and just a few months before Dr. Condon asked for about a quarter of a million dollars more to continue his work.

This statement upset many of the UFO societies. Then came another blow for those expecting an unbiased report. A memo written by Robert Low, the project administrator, was smuggled out. It was written when the UFO project was under consideration by the university, of which Low was Special Assistant to the Vice-President and Dean of Faculties. He wrote: "The trick would be, I think, to describe the project so that, to the public, it would appear a totally objective study, but to the scientific community, would present the image of a group of nonbelievers trying their best to be objective but having an almost zero expectation of finding a saucer."

It seemed that the report's conclusions were being shaped even before the university received the contract. Dr. J. Allen

Above left: is it a hovering UFO? Above: no, simply a metal plate. The photographer spins the plate into the air, snaps his picture, and he has his "flying saucer." Among the UFO pictures submitted to investigators have been many hoaxes as elementary as this one—a fact which skeptics are quick to point to as unfavorable evidence of the kind of person who is likely to make a UFO report.

Hynek, the astronomer who worked closely with Project Blue Book for many years, has this to say about the early days of the Colorado project: "I remember my own dismay when, on the occasion of my visit to the committee, when the project was scarcely two weeks old, Low outlined on the blackboard for us the form the report would take, what the probable chapter headings would be, how much space should be devoted to each chapter, with an implied attitude that he had decided already what the substance and tone of the report would be."

Dr. Condon has dismissed the significance of the Low memo, explaining that he did not see it until 18 months after it was written, and that he disagreed with some points in it including the suggestion that the study should concentrate on psychological rather than physical aspects of flying saucer sightings. Nevertheless, since other commitments often kept Dr. Condon away from the project, Low was the man who, to quote Dr. Hynek again, "became the actual pilot of the Colorado UFO ship." Dr. Condon was sufficiently incensed by the disclosure of the Low memo, however, to dismiss the two committee members he regarded as responsible for the leak. They were pro-UFO, and without them the Colorado "UFO ship" could look forward to a smooth voyage with its nonbelieving passengers.

The final report of the Colorado UFO project is a massive tome—965 pages in its paperback version—which makes daunting reading for all but the most enthusiastic scientists and UFO followers. Seemingly in a helpful way, the report has its

Above: British policemen warily inspect one of six bleeping disks found in fields across southern England one morning in September 1967. Police took them away, and a bomb disposal expert blew one up—but only found a small loudspeaker, batteries, and several gallons of flour paste.
Below: these two students, Chris Southall and David Harrison, admitted they had fabricated the "saucers" from the mold they are holding—as a fund-raising stunt.

Below: Paul Trent, a farmer of McMinnville, Oregon. He and his wife sighted a UFO in May 1950. His wife saw it first while feeding the rabbits at the back of the house, and shouted to him. He grabbed a camera in time to be able to get two pictures.

Above: Trent's first picture. The analysis of his negatives showed they had not been tampered with. Elaborate geometric and light calculations showed both pictures were consistent with each other and the time of day. Even the Condon report, having considered the possibility of a model hung from the wires, came to the conclusion that "this is one of the few UFO reports in which all factors investigated appear to be consistent with the assertion that an extraordinary flying object . . . flew within sight of two witnesses."

conclusions at the beginning so that readers not prepared to plough through acres of type can learn them in just over 40 pages. However, readers who give up at that point will be sadly misled, for Dr. Condon's summary avoids mentioning any of the outstanding cases that remained unsolved after the in-depth study by the Colorado scientists. Closer scrutiny of the entire report shows that the findings are based on a study of only 90 sightings out of a potential 25,000 available to them. What is more, these 90 cases are not the best or most puzzling. They are a curious cross-section, including an attempt to rendezvous with a flying saucer which, it was said, would be landing at a specific time and place. It did not turn up! Other cases included lights and objects that any experienced investigator could explain away in minutes. In fact, 14 of the cases had already been evaluated as misperceptions by Project Blue Book.

Dr. Hynek, who is not a believer in the extraterrestrial origin of flying saucers, makes this observation about the Colorado findings: "The report opened with a singularly slanted summary by Dr. Condon, which adroitly avoided mentioning that there was embodied within the bowels of the report a remaining mystery; the committee had been unable to furnish adequate explanations for more than a quarter of the cases examined."

The press greeted the report as the UFO enthusiasts had expected. Basing their headlines on the summary, they announced: "Flying Saucers Do Not Exist—Official." The serious saucer investigators read between the lines and found what *they* expected: confirmation that UFOs exist. Many also regarded the discrepancies and method of presentation of the report as further evidence that the truth about UFOs is being hidden from the public.

The Colorado investigation did nothing to solve the UFO dilemma in general terms. From the Air Force's point of view, however, it was a useful exercise. Largely upon the recommendation of the Colorado team, the USAF terminated its official investigation of flying saucers in December 1969 with the closure of Project Blue Book.

Since then the public has been faced with a new dilemma. To whom should they report a flying saucer if they see one? Soon after the closure of Project Blue Book a letter went out from the Pentagon specifying: "The Aerospace Defense Command (ADC) is charged with the responsibility for aerospace defense of the United States. . . . Consequently, ADC is responsible for unknown aerial phenomena reported in any manner, and the provisions of Joint Army–Navy–Air Force publication (JANAP–146) provide for the processing of reports received from nonmilitary sources."

So, though flying saucers do not exist in the eyes of the Air Force, it would still like to know when people see them. However, under JANAP–146 heavy penalties are imposed on anyone disclosing information received about unidentified objects. So UFOs are still enveloped in a cloak of secrecy—or a conspiracy of silence.

Below: Condon made little attempt to disguise his skepticism about the reality of UFOs—which did nothing to allay the belief in a conspiracy of silence—and was an easy target for satire. This 1967 Oliphant cartoon from the *Denver Post* plays on his attitude.

Chariots
of the Gods

In the Peruvian Andes in South America lies the arid plain of Nazca, a strip about 37 miles long and a mile wide. The extra-ordinary feature of the land is that it is covered with strange geometric patterns formed by deep straight furrows that expose the yellowish subsoil. Some of the lines run parallel for miles. Others intersect or join to make large trapezoidal shapes. Among the lines numerous animal figures have been etched, the biggest being 275 yards at its widest point. But the odd thing about the figures and the geometric patterns is that they can only be properly appreciated from a height—for example, by someone flying over

Are the inhabitants of this world part of a breeding experiment supervised by intergalactic space people who dart in and out of our planet to check on its progress? According to the theories of Swiss author Erich von Däniken, that may well have been the case. Above: von Däniken, giving a lecture on his view of history. Right: a strange ceramic figure found in South America. This is the kind of evidence von Däniken uses to argue that space people visited the Earth in antiquity.

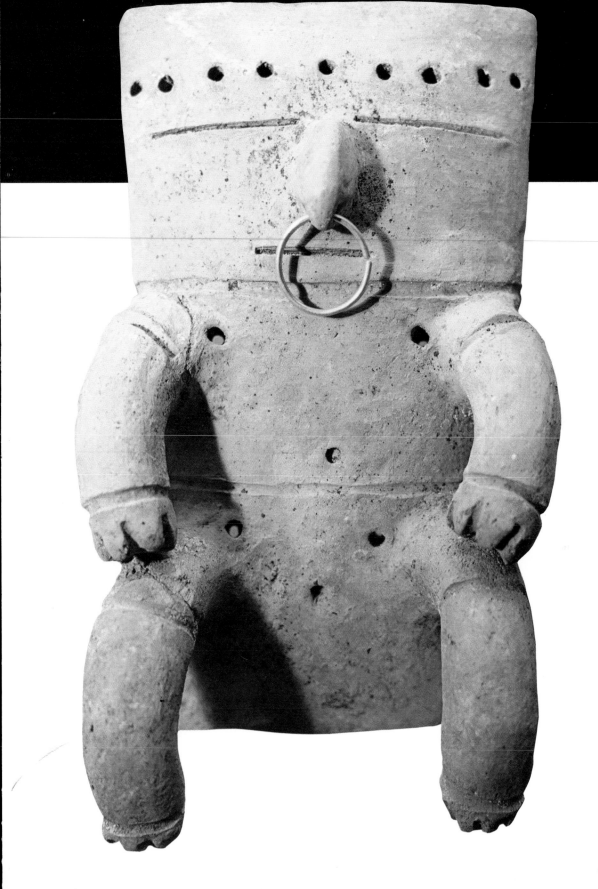

"Why should the Incas need such complex roads...?"

Below: an artifact of gold from Colombia, similar to many gold objects that have been found in other places in South America. Some theorists have claimed that it is a model of a delta-winged aircraft with cockpit, windshield, a flanged tail, and elevators.

Above right: one of several sites near Nazca, Peru said to be landing fields for spacecraft by von Däniken. Since they can only be plotted from the air, he believes they were built with guidance from an aircraft. One of his critics remarked that an aircraft needing the length of some of the runways —which extend for miles—would have had impossibly bad brakes.

in a plane. Yet the people who planned the patterns and animal figures centuries and centuries ago were not able to fly. Why, then, are the designs so obscure at ground level? What were they for? What do they mean?

One archeological theory is that the lines are Inca roads. But why should the Incas need such a complex system of parallel and intersecting roads, all of which terminate at the edge of the plain? Another supposition is that they are irrigation channels. But what purpose do the vast animal figures serve between the channels in that case? Perhaps more convincing is the belief that the lines represent some astronomical plan that may in some way be linked with a calendar. By far the boldest idea, however, and the one that has attracted most public speculation, comes from the Swiss author Erich von Däniken. He believes that the markings were designed to be seen from the air because the plain of Nazca was intended to be an airport. His theory is that many thousands of years ago inhabitants of another planet landed

Airfield for the Gods?

In the 1930s some mysterious markings were discovered on a plain near Nazca, Peru. They consisted of long straight lines in a geometric pattern, with enormous animal figures between them. One of the most amazing things about these markings was that they had to be seen from the air to get a full overall picture. Yet archeologists agreed that they were made long before aircraft existed. Were the lines ancient roads or irrigation canals as most scientists suggested? Or was the layout an airfield built by space people way in the past? This is the view of Erich von Däniken, whose writings on spacecraft landings in antiquity have been a sensational success.

Von Däniken believes that beings of superior intelligence landed near Nazca from space and built an airfield for future use. These "gods" were admired by tribes who saw them, and who hoped for their return. When the gods didn't come back, the tribes began to extend the airfield to entice them. First they just added lines. Then another generation thought of adding more lines according to the stars. Still later generations did the drawings as special landing signals.

That, von Däniken claims, is how Nazca became an airfield for the gods.

their spacecraft on the Nazca plain and improvised an airfield there.

Von Däniken has become world-famous on the basis of such bold suggestions. A self-taught man, he offers rather startling theories to explain the numerous mysteries that perplex minds molded by more orthodox teachings. He believes that all over the world evidence can be found to show that beings from outer space have walked on earth and talked to humans.

Nazca is just one piece of his jigsaw puzzle. He has filled four books with the other pieces, and his globetrotting research continues in an attempt to provide conclusive proof. These books, *Chariots of the Gods?, Return to the Stars, Gold of the Gods,* and *In Search of Ancient Gods* had worldwide sales approaching 30 million in 1975. The remarkable appeal of his theories has been diagnosed by skeptics as "Dänikenitis." But strong criticism of many of his statements by authorities has done little so far to diminish the popularity of his beliefs.

Von Däniken differs from so many classical scholars in his insistence that the myths and legends of our distant past should be taken more literally. He believes that our own tentative steps in space exploration have added a new dimension to our past so that we can now examine the stories of our earliest recorded history in the light of our new experiences. For example, why is it that the myths of most cultures refer to gods coming from the skies? Until von Däniken put forward his theories, this idea was regarded as symbolic. But according to the Swiss author, if another race of beings had landed on Earth in the past, the description of their visit would tally exactly with what we find in these myths. He believes that latent memories of those visits have driven us to mount massive space programs to reestablish contact.

The controversial writer offers an additional and even more sensational reason for our deep-seated drive to reach Outer Space. The space visitors, he says, are our forefathers. *Homo sapiens* was created by the "gods" by an artificial mutation providing a cross breed between themselves and the more humanlike apes who populated the earth at that time.

Von Däniken's hypothesis is based on evidence like the ancient stone relief discovered in Palenque, Mexico in 1935. This is described by him in *Chariots of the Gods?* in these words:

"There sits a human being, with the upper part of his body bent forward like a racing motor-cyclist; today any child would identify his vehicle as a rocket. It is pointed at the front, then changes to strangely grooved indentations like inlet ports, widens out and terminates at the tail in a darting flame. The crouching being himself is manipulating a number of undefinable controls and has the heel of his left foot on a kind of pedal. His clothing is appropriate: short trousers with a broad belt, a jacket with a modern Japanese opening at the neck and closely fitting bands at arms and legs . . . And there [is the headgear] with the usual indentations and tubes, and something like antenna on top. Our space traveler—he is clearly depicted as one—is not only bent forward tensely, he is also looking intently at an apparatus hanging in front of his face."

The author sees other relics of the past in the same light. Almost every ancient figure depicted with strange headgear is described by him as a spaceman equipped with antenna. To argue that it is simply a ritual mask or headdress—as many specialists do—does not dissuade von Däniken. He asks why, if this is so, the masks or headdresses were shaped in that way in the first place. He suggests that it is a ritual tradition specifically designed to keep alive our memory of space visitors.

To support his case von Däniken cites rock drawings all over the world. In the Tassili mountains in the Algerian Sahara, for example, there are hundreds of figures that according to von Däniken are wearing round helmets with antenna on their heads, and seem to be floating weightlessly in space. One particular drawing has a more specific interpretation for him. It is of a sphere with a series of four concentric circles. At the top of the sphere there seems to be a hatch with an aerial protruding, and from the side two hands are stretched out. Accompanying the sphere are five floating figures with tight fitting helmets. Von

Left: Temple of the Inscriptions in Palenque, Mexico. It has the famous stone relief that von Däniken says was of an astronaut.

Below left: a photograph of the stone relief. The sculpture is in a spot so narrow that there is no room to get a picture head-on. All photographs of it therefore have a distorted appearance.

Above: a drawing of the Palenque relief. Von Däniken says that the pointed vehicle ending in a tail is clearly a rocket, and points out that the figure handling it has the right clothing for space travel.

Däniken concludes that these paintings represent the memories of a visit to earth by beings from outer space, handed down for many generations.

If our planet has been the temporary home of superior beings from another planet, we would expect to find more substantial proof than rock paintings. The Nazca site has been offered as evidence, and so has the mysterious plateau of El Enladrillado in Chile. This was rediscovered in 1968, and has provided archeologists with yet another puzzle. The two-mile-long plateau can only be reached by a three-hour journey on horseback. When visitors arrive they are greeted by an astonishing sight. The ground is covered with more than 200 giant rectangular stone blocks which are extremely smooth of surface. They range from 12 to 16 feet high and 20 to 30 feet long. Exactly 233 of them have been grouped to form what resembles an amphitheater at a glance. Who could have hewn and shaped such enormous blocks with such precision, and how could they have managed to bring them to such an inaccessible spot? Why were they there, and what were they for? Archeologists have not yet come up with a convincing explanation. Von Däniken says that a strip of ground of about a thousand yards long among the huge stones was a landing strip. According to the Chilean newspaper *El Mercurio*, the leader of the scientific expedition to investigate the plateau in 1968, Humberto Sarnataro Bounaud, said he believed that the stones were the work of an ancient unknown culture of advanced technology, because the natives of the region were incapable of such achievements. He also observed that whoever was responsible knew that the plateau would make a first-class landing ground for all kinds of flying craft. If this were so, the 233 symmetrically arranged stone blocks may have been visual landing sights for aircraft rather than an amphitheater.

Could superior beings with flying machines have shaped the blocks and positioned them, either to serve as a sign to aircraft or for some other reason? Our planet is scattered with strange and enormous buildings and monoliths. We find it hard to understand how they were erected or why they were positioned in certain sites. On tiny Easter Island 2250 miles from the coast of Chile are hundreds of gigantic statues, some between 33 and 66 feet high. They are a great puzzle. Who carved them? Why were they erected on this remote and inaccessible place? Questions also remain about how the Egyptian and Mayan pyramids were constructed. Nor do we yet know the meaning of giant stone circles like Stonehenge in the South of England.

If, as von Däniken suggests, a race of extraterrestrials was responsible for building many of these monuments then the mystery is to some extent solved. They would choose sites that marked places of special importance to them or served as landing strips.

Tiahuanaco is another South American wonder to which von Däniken refers. It is the site of a huge ancient city on a plateau at a height of 13,000 feet. The oxygen level is very low and working conditions must have been extremely hard. Despite this, enormous buildings of some kind were constructed. The walls consist of huge blocks of sandstone weighing a hundred tons according to von Däniken. These are topped with other

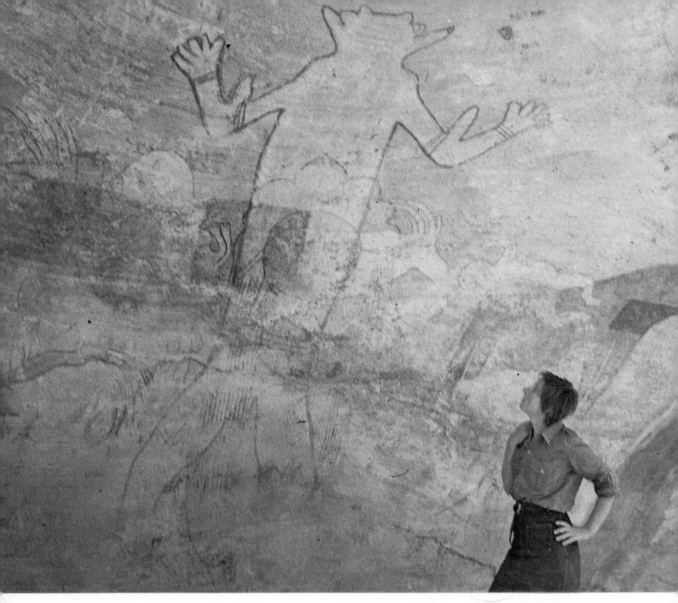

blocks weighing 60 tons. Large squared stones with smooth surfaces are neatly fitted together and fastened with copper clamps. One of the greatest archeological wonders of South America is also found in Tiahuanaco. It is the Gate of the Sun. This gigantic 10-ton sculpture, carved out of a single block, tells the story of a golden spaceship that came from the stars. It carried Oryana, the woman who became the Great Mother of the Earth. She had four webbed fingers on each hand. After giving birth to 70 children, she returned to the stars.

Also found at Tiahuanaco was a calendar, which von Däniken describes as giving the position of the moon for every hour, taking the rotation of the earth into account. Still another extraordinary discovery was the Great Idol, a block of red sandstone over 24 feet long. It is inscribed with hundreds of symbols which, according to the book *The Great Idol of Tiahuanaco* by H. S. Bellamy and P. Allan, records an enormous body of astronomical knowledge based on a round Earth. Where did such knowledge come from?

To support his theories von Däniken cites a fascinating

Above: a rock painting in the Tassili mountains, which lie in the Algerian Sahara. According to von Däniken the main figure, which seems to float weightlessly in empty space, was a Martian on a visit to Earth long years ago.

Right: a figure of the type known as Wondjina to the Australian Aborigines who treasure them. They appear in rock paintings, upright and staring out from the walls. Could the curious ornament on their head be a helmet? An odd thing about the marks on this drawing is that the hieroglyphics are the same as those George Adamski claims he received from a Venusian who met with him in the California desert in 1952.

discovery in China. In 1938 the Chinese archeologist Chi Pu Tei discovered a series of graves arranged in rows in the mountain caves of the Sino-Tibetan border district. The cave walls were decorated with figures in round helmets and the sun, moon, and stars linked together by groups of small dots. Chi Pu Tei and his assistants managed to salvage from the graves 716 granite plates, about two centimeters thick. According to von Däniken, these looked much like our long-playing records. The stone plates had a hole in the center from which a double-grooved incised script spiraled outward to the edge.

The disturbing thing about the graves was that, whereas the skeletons were small in stature, the skulls were large and broad. Chi Pu Tei suggested that these were the remains of a now extinct species of mountain ape—though apes are not known for making graves, particularly in neat rows. Clearly they were not responsible for the stone plates. The archeologist suggested that the plates must have been put there at a later date by others of a different culture.

For 20 years experts tried to solve the riddle of the stone plates. Then in 1962 Professor Tsum Um Nui of the Academy of Prehistoric Research in Peking claimed he was able to decipher parts of the scripts. The Academy had doubts about the scripts and the astonishing story they told, so it refused to publish the findings. In 1963, when Tsum Um Nui had support from four other scientists, he published the results himself. The plates, he revealed, told of an aircraft that crashed on the third planet [Earth] 12,000 years ago. It did not have enough power to leave this world again and the people on board did not have the means to build a new aircraft. They tried to make friends with the mountain inhabitants but when some of them were hunted down and killed, the remainder hid themselves in the caves.

If space visitors wanted to explore our earth without being molested it seems likely that they would take shelter in natural caves, or even build their own subterranean world. It was this belief that took von Däniken to Ecuador to meet the discoverer

Right: another of the ancient Mexican stone figures—this one on a monolith—which von Däniken believes bears all the advanced technical equipment of the modern astronaut. He uses this to support his contention that these ancient civilizations were in contact with intelligent beings of considerable technological achievements.

Around the world are gigantic old monuments that modern scholars have only been partly able to explain why and how they were built. Above: the pyramid of Cheops. Why did the Pharaoh build it there? Left: the ambiguous stone monoliths of Stonehenge in rural England. Below: the Easter Island statues. How and why were they erected?

of a huge complex of underground passages and halls beneath the South American continent.

Juan Moricz, an Argentinian, claims to be the legal owner of part of this strange underground world. But because he is convinced of the incalculable cultural value of his find he asked the State of Ecuador to take control and set up a scientific commission to study the area. No official response was forthcoming after Moricz deposited his legal title-deed, and the discovery awaits detailed investigation. But Moricz agreed to take von Däniken into the passages and show him some of their treasures. This experience is described in *The Gold of the Gods*.

The passages are not in a rough natural state. The walls and ceilings are smooth, and all form perfect right angles. One wonders what tools can have been used to carve these tunnels which, Moricz claims, run for thousands of miles beneath the earth's surface. The discoverer led von Däniken along the passages and into a vast hall "as big as the hangar of a jumbo jet," with galleries branching off it. They continued through another passage and into a perfectly proportioned but gigantic hall. In the center was a table and chairs. They appeared to be made of some kind of plastic but were as strong and as heavy as steel.

"There were animals behind the chairs: saurians, elephants, lions, crocodiles, jaguars, camels, bears, monkeys, bison, and wolves, with snails and crabs crawling about between them. Apparently they had been cast in moulds and there was no logical sequence about their arrangement . . . The whole thing was like a fantastic zoo and what is more all the animals were made of solid gold."

The most astonishing treasure was housed in the same animal hall. It was a library of metal plaques and metal leaves only millimeters thick. Von Däniken, who examined them, says that most of them measured about 3 feet 2 inches by 1 foot 7 inches. The metal was unusual, he says, for the leaves stood upright without buckling, in spite of their size and thinness. They stood next to each other like bound pages of giant folios, and each was covered with writing that looked as if it had been stamped on by a machine. He estimated that there were between two and three thousand of these metal pages in an unknown writing. Von Däniken declares: "This metal library was created to outlast the ages, to remain legible for eternity." He believes the writing to be the oldest in existence on this planet, perhaps containing a history of man from his earliest days—and the visitation of extraterrestrial beings who left this permanent record of their intervention in the development of life on Earth.

In *Chariots of the Gods?* von Däniken offers this idea of what may have happened when an unknown spaceship discovered our planet:

"The crew of the spaceship soon found out that the Earth had all the prerequisites for intelligent life to develop. Obviously the 'man' of those times was not *homo sapiens*, but something rather different. The spacemen artificially fertilized some female members of this species, put them into a deep sleep, so ancient legends say, and departed. Thousands of years later the space travelers returned and found scattered specimens of the genus *homo sapiens*. They repeated their breeding experiment several

Easter Island Riddle

The colossal stone statues of Easter Island in the South Pacific have astounded and puzzled explorers, anthropologists, and ordinary tourists for hundreds of years. No one can explain how such huge stone slabs could have been carried from the only quarry on the island some distance away, nor how the volcanic stone could have been worked with the small primitive tools that are the only ones ever found on the island. Even more mysterious is the question of why the statues have long straight noses, narrow lips, and low foreheads when no island dwellers—nor any of their ancestors—look like that.

Erich von Däniken has a theory that fits in with his ideas about unexplained statuary, drawings, and monuments all around the world. The Easter Island figures, he says, were the work of space visitors.

According to von Däniken the space people were stranded on the island through some mishap. While waiting to be rescued—and perhaps as a signal to their rescuers—they built some gigantic statues and lined them up where they could be seen from afar. They could do all this easily because of advanced technology.

The gods left Easter Island suddenly, von Däniken suggests, which is why some of the statues remained unfinished.

Above: the Gate of the Sun, part of the remains of the ancient city of Tiahuanaco in Bolivia. Said to have been carved out of a single block of stone, it weighs 10 tons. Forty-eight square figures in three rows surround a flying god. According to von Däniken, legend says that the city was created by a woman from a golden spaceship, who came from the stars to become the Great Mother of the earth. She gave birth to 70 earth children and then returned to her starry home. For von Däniken this legend supports his argument that giant projects like the Gate of the Sun were constructed with the aid of interplanetary visitors.

times until finally they produced a creature intelligent enough to have the rules of society imparted to it."

He finds support for this theory in the story of Adam and Eve. Man existed, but woman had to be created. Is this a symbolic way of explaining that men came to the Earth and created a species? Why did they use Adam's rib? Von Däniken asks why foreign intelligences with a highly developed science who knew about the immune biological reactions of bones could not have used Adam's marrow as a cell culture and brought male sperm to development in it.

As von Däniken's books have flourished, so have the theories of this prolific Swiss author changed to fit new discoveries. He has tried to make every modern mystery fit into his extraterrestrial jigsaw. He flies around the world to study archeological and historical wonders for himself. By the time *The Gold of the Gods* appeared his jigsaw was virtually complete. He believes that the prehistory of humankind happened something like the following:

In the distant past a battle occurred in our galaxy between humanlike intelligences. The losers escaped in a spaceship. To deceive their opponents they landed on Earth, a far from ideal planet, where they had to wear helmets and breathing apparatus until they accustomed themselves to the air. They then set up technical stations and transmitters on a different planet, then known as the fifth planet, and sent out coded reports. Their trick was successful.

The victors of the galactic battle were fooled into believing that those they had defeated had established a base on the fifth planet, and annihilated it in a gigantic explosion. This accounts for the existence of a planetoid belt containing thousands of lumps of stone between the present day fourth and fifth planets, Mars and Jupiter.

Meanwhile the space visitors burrowed deep into the ground on Earth and made tunnel systems that not only hid them from their pursuers, but also protected them from a general air attack. The victors, believing they had destroyed their enemies, withdrew to their home planet. But the imbalance in our solar system caused by the destruction of a planet made the Earth's axis move a few degrees out of position, and brought about the floods and deluges which are part of the legends of people all over the world.

When the space visitors eventually emerged from their magnificently built underground world they began creating intelligence on earth, using their knowledge of molecular biology. Taking the most advanced species of ape then in existence, they used it to create man in their own image. They laid down strict laws to ensure that the new breed remained pure, and they wiped out those who did not live up to their expectations. They were looked upon as gods by the Earth creatures. After generations of breeding, man as we know him emerged on our planet. That, in essence, is von Däniken's strange hypothesis.

No one would deny the right of revolutionaries and visionaries to hypothesize to their heart's content, even on matters of such fundamental importance as human origin. But scholars are always wary of the way supporting evidence can be bent to fit even the wildest theory, and they have accused von Däniken of such behavior. It is said that he has plundered almost every culture to find proof, and that he has disregarded all the facts that tend to disprove his claims. After a group of academics studied his first book *Chariots of the Gods?*, their often amusing comments were edited by E. W. Castle and B. B. Thiering and published under the title *Some Trust in Chariots!* They point out numerous fallacies on which von Däniken's theories are based, and on the basis of the most modern findings in the realms of history, archeology, engineering, and religion, offer more mundane explanations for many of the feats accredited by von Däniken to the hypothetical space visitors.

In their introduction the editors put the case against von Däniken in these words: "Some of his 'facts' are false and his arguments from these 'facts' are not acceptable arguments at all." It seems that von Däniken can be attacked at many levels. Gordon Whittaker, an expert on the Aztec civilization, points out a mistake that could have been avoided by a quick perusal of some museum catalog. Von Däniken asserts that the giant heads sculpted by the Olmec people of Mexico are too heavy to ever be moved from their site because no bridge could stand their weight. But Whittaker shows that, not only do several museums possess such heads in their collections, but also one of the heads

Below: the Great Idol monolith at Tiahuanaco. The symbols which decorate the surface have been interpreted as recording an incredibly detailed knowledge of astronomy—astonishing in view of what could be expected of that period and in that isolated place.

Above: a reconstruction of how a step pyramid may have been built, according to one theory of orthodox archeology. Although von Däniken seems to think that rope did not exist, and that there was no wood in Egypt to use for rollers, there are in fact examples of Egyptian rope in existence. Moreover, records of cargoes of imported wood are well known to scholars. Von Däniken also appears to be mistaken about the weight of the blocks. He estimates the weight of each block as being 12 tons, but most of the blocks really weighed only about $2\frac{1}{2}$ tons each.

was recently transported thousands of miles for an exhibition at the Metropolitan Museum of Art in New York. At a different level, Whittaker also demonstrates that von Däniken's belief that the Easter Island inhabitants could not have carved and erected their giant statues unaided is ill founded. The statues are not the only huge monuments found on Polynesian islands, and there are native accounts of how they were moved with ropes and stone rollers.

Another contributor to this fascinating book that tries to take von Däniken's theories apart piece by piece is Professor Basil Hennessy from the University of Sydney, Australia. He refers to von Däniken's "fascinating collection of unsupported, undigested, disconnected and often inaccurate claims," and then goes on to show how seriously the Swiss author errs in his facts. For example, the Great Pyramid of Giza is said by von Däniken to weigh 31,200,000 tons. Professor Hennessy points out that there are an estimated 2,300,000 blocks known to weigh an average of $2\frac{1}{2}$ tons for a total of 5,750,000 tons. Moreover the blocks are made of soft limestone rather than hard granite as von Däniken suggests, and the stone was quarried in the immediate vicinity of the pyramids and not miles away. The blocks were moved into position by rope, which von Däniken believes was nonexistent at that time but which can be seen in abundance in a number of museums. Von Däniken says that there was no wood to make rollers for moving the massive blocks, but Professor Hennessy reveals that the ancient Egyptians imported vast quantities of wood from other countries.

Dr. A. D. Crown of the Department of Semitic Studies at the University of Sydney challenges von Däniken on his theories about the Piri Re'is map, said to have been drawn by Admiral Piri at the beginning of the 16th century. Quoting American cartographers, von Däniken stated that when the map was constructed on a grid and transferred to a modern globe it was absolutely accurate. It showed the Mediterranean and Dead Seas, the coasts of North and South America, and even the contours of the Antarctic. The Piri Re'is map is said to have contained details of interiors as well as coasts, including the mountain ranges of the Antarctic which were not discovered until 1952 by echosounding apparatus. Von Däniken declares that aerial photographs must have been used as the basis for the Piri Re'is map. He suggests that these photographs were taken centuries ago from an aircraft or spaceship hovering high above Cairo. Copies were made and handed down, and copies of these copies were made, and so on. According to von Däniken the Piri Re'is map is a copy of a copy of a copy, but it is originally based on aerial photography.

Dr. Crown agrees that the map is impressive, but he shows conclusively that its origin is not a mystery. Nor is it necessary to believe in aerial photography to explain its existence. It does not show as much as von Däniken believes it shows, and what it does show was known to experienced mariners of the early 16th century, he says.

In a review of von Däniken's book *In Search of Ancient Gods*, Jacquetta Hawkes in the English *Sunday Times* of September 15, 1974, points out an error about the position of our galaxy that

Above: a museum exhibit of South American carvings. The one on the right is an Olmec head of the kind that von Däniken says, "they can only be admired on the sites where they were found, for . . . no bridge in the country could stand the weight of the colossi." Challengers of von Däniken ask him how, in that case, the carvings were brought to the museum. Left: an Easter Island statue in the British Museum. Von Däniken points out that it would have been impossible for Easter Island's small population to have carved and erected hundreds of these strange figures. However, a historian argues that the figures are typical of religious carvings on other Polynesian islands. He also argues with the point that the job of carving and erecting was not done overnight, but over a long period of time, using tools that are still found in quantity on the island. Inhabitants could describe exactly how the giant figures were put into position to anthropologist Thor Heyerdahl when he investigated the matter.

Left: the Piri Re'is map, said to have belonged to a Turkish Navy admiral, discovered in the Topkapi Seraglio in 1935—not in the 18th century as von Däniken apparently believes. According to von Däniken this map shows mountain ranges of Antarctica now so deeply covered with snow that it requires echo-sounding apparatus to map them. He also says that this is an aerial view, which required the help of space people in aircraft. Right: an azimuthal projection based on Cairo and proposed by von Däniken as the one used in the Piri Re'is map. Azimuths project the curved surface of a globe onto a flat surface based on a given center, so distortions always occur. However, Dr. A. D. Crown of the University of Sydney points out that the distortion cited by von Däniken to explain the peculiar length of South America on the Piri Re'is map would not occur in an azimuthal projection based on Cairo.

Above: the black line indicates the area that the Piri Re'is map covers as Dr. Crown sees it. The coasts of South America accurately mapped were already known to cartographers in 1513, when the map was drawn. Antarctica, ice-covered or not, does not appear on Dr. Crown's projection.

occurs on the very first page of the book. A second error concerns the dating of Tiahuanaco as 600 B.C. by von Däniken, whereas it should be A.D. 600. These, she wrote, are just "two out of the scores of simple errors scattered on almost every page." She also points out that more than 40 of the photographs and illustrations in the book are of well-known forgeries.

Experts are not always right of course. Besides there are also some experts who support von Däniken's beliefs. However, few would defend his rather reckless methods of research and presentation, and if his hypothesis is correct, it will require far more proof. Yet it has to be admitted that the possibility that Earth has been visited by advanced beings is a real one. There could be many inhabited planets where life developed much earlier than it has on this planet. If their technological advances occurred at a similar rate to ours but a few thousand years earlier, they may well have solved the problems of traversing vast expanses of the Universe. If so, they could have left some evidence of their visit, just as we from Earth have done on our own uninhabited satellite. Perhaps in fact the space visitors have never left us but have kept their distance and monitor our progress from the skies. Could it be that we are no more than an intergalactic breeding experiment?

Whatever the physical proof—or lack of it—as regards space visitors and human origins, the record shows that strange objects have been reported in our skies since the earliest recorded history. Until a logical explanation can be offered for these—and their modern equivalent the flying saucers—we should probably keep an open mind about Erich von Däniken's sensational theories.

4

Spacecraft in Early Times

Over a thousand strange objects were reported in the skies above Sweden in a 12-month period. That is remarkable in itself. What makes it more remarkable is that it occurred in 1946—the year before flying saucers hit the world headlines. It could not, therefore, be explained away as mass hysteria, though the Swedish press did take up the story and the objects became known as "ghost rockets." They were usually seen at night, and some accounts describe them as cigar-shaped with orange flames issuing from the tail. In the period from July 9 to July 30 alone, the Swedish military received more than 600 reports,

Right: spaceships in ancient Egypt—a pre-von Däniken view from an American science fiction magazine published in 1948. Strange flying objects were reported long before Arnold saw his flying saucers in 1947, and the witnesses form an oddly assorted crew—from Old Testament prophets to a Kansas farmer. They even include Christopher Columbus as he sailed the Atlantic Ocean.

"UFOs have been with us as long as man has been able to record his past..."

Below: an illustration for Jules Verne's *The Clipper of the Clouds* (1886). Robur, the hero of the story, has a shadowy background and unimaginable wealth. He builds a giant airship, which takes him around the world and into a series of incredible adventures. Using the technology of his age, Verne clearly visualized Robur's craft —the *aeronef*—as a combination of an airship and a seagoing vessel.

mostly of fast-moving colored lights in the night sky.

These UFOs caused serious concern at the time in both the United States and Scandinavia. It was feared that German scientists in the Soviet-occupied zone of Germany were developing and testing a new secret weapon. Even before this, during World War II, there had been reports of UFOs seen mainly at night. Each side had found them perplexing, and each had thought that they were secret weapons being developed by the other. They were given the name of "foo fighters" by British and American pilots who encountered them. What impressed airmen was that these small colored lights appeared to be under intelligent control.

A spate of reports of foo fighters started to come in about November 1944. They were encountered by night fighters flying over the Rhine north of Strasbourg. Typical of the accounts is this report filed by Lieutenant David McFalls, and published in Harold Wilkins' book *Flying Saucers from the Moon.*

"At 0600 near Hagenau, at 10,000 feet altitude, two very bright lights climbed toward us from the ground. They leveled off and stayed on the tail of our plane. They were huge, bright orange lights. They stayed there for two minutes. On my tail all the time. They were under perfect control. Then they turned away from us, and the fire seemed to go out."

Others reported even more incredible encounters. The foo fighters would sometimes race ahead or fly abreast of aircraft, and then drop behind and follow the tail. When the pilots made abrupt changes of course, the balls of fire remained on their tails, in one case for as long as 75 minutes. This was wartime, so the aircraft showed no lights. The foo fighters were certainly not reflections of the planes.

It is understandable that these UFOs and the ghost rockets seen over Sweden two years later should have been regarded as a secret weapon developed by the enemy. But history has shown that they did not belong to either side. History also shows that UFOs have been with us for as long as man has been able to record his past, and probably before then as well. As a result "ufologists"—the popular name for UFO researchers—have plundered the history books and produced a profusion of volumes with titles like *The Bible and Flying Saucers, God Drives a Flying Saucer,* and *Flying Saucers Through the Ages.*

If modern science has been unable to prove the reality of UFOs with radar and photographic evidence, then clearly a rummage through ancient records is not going to provide proof either. The witnesses are no longer around to be questioned. The statements they made, or that are attributed to them, are usually highly colored but insufficiently detailed to enable us to make a positive identification at this late stage. In most cases, however, we can rule out satellites, aircraft, or the other products of modern technology that feature so prominently today as the explanation for many UFOs.

One of the most remarkable early UFO periods was 1896–7, when craft resembling airships were seen by many people in different parts of the United States. They were usually described as cigar-shaped, and often the reports spoke of powerful searchlights aimed at the ground from these aerial visitors. Most witnesses assumed they were man-made, but although airships were certainly at the design stage, there is no evidence that any were yet in operation at that time.

The 19th-century sky visitors provoked startling headlines, and with good reason. For example, a Kansas farmer, Alexander Hamilton, reported an encounter that would make front page news in any newspaper even today. He was awakened by the noise of his cattle at 10:30 p.m. on April 19, 1897, and on going to investigate he saw "an airship slowly descending upon my cow lot about 40 rods from the house." He called his son and a tenant, and the three men rushed outside with axes. The airship was now hovering just 30 feet above the ground. It was cigar-shaped, about 300 feet long, and had a transparent, brilliantly lit undercarriage. In a sworn statement Hamilton reported that the airship carried "six of the strangest beings I ever saw." They turned a beam of light directly on him. Then a large turbine wheel, about 30 feet in diameter, began to buzz as it revolved slowly "and the vessel rose as lightly as a bird."

When the airship reached an estimated height of 300 feet it stopped and hovered. The three men saw that a thick cable had been put around a two-year-old heifer's neck, and the occupants began to hoist it aboard. The airship then flew off as the witnesses watched in amazement. Next morning Hamilton could not believe what he had seen, and he went in search of the animal. He learned that a neighboring farmer had found the hide, head, and legs of the butchered heifer in his field.

Hamilton ended his statement with these words: "I don't know whether they are devils or angels, or what; but we all saw

Below: a photograph of the first British airship for military purposes, shown under test in 1907. It is at anchor near Farnborough, England. In the beginning of the 20th century the airship was the most technologically advanced product of aeronautics. Perhaps not surprisingly, the scattered reports of UFO sightings during that period most often described the objects as similar to airships.

Left: dark balls in the sky, shown in a 16th-century woodcut. They were seen in Basel, Switzerland in August 1566, and resembled the blood-red round objects sighted in Nürnberg four years previously.

Below: the English astronomer Edmund Halley. It was he who predicted the reappearance of the comet that was subsequently given his name. Halley also reported two sightings of UFOs. One of them he saw in 1677, a year after an Italian sighting was reported to him, and the other— a particularly bright one—he observed 39 years later in 1716.

Left: Christopher Columbus on the deck of the Santa Maria. On the night before the historic sighting of the New World, Columbus saw a glimmering light at a distance. He called one of his crew members to observe it with him. The light vanished and reappeared several times during the night.

them, and my whole family saw the ship, and I don't want any more to do with them."

The *Colony Free Press* of Kansas soon had this explanation for its readers: "The *Free Press . . .* is *now* of the opinion that the airship is not of *this world*, but is probably operated by a party of scientists from the planet Mars, who are out, either on a lark, or a tour of inspection of the solar system in the cause of science."

So the Martians were thought to be responsible even in the 19th century!

José Bonilla, a Mexican astronomer, enjoyed a UFO show all his own in August 1883. He was taking photographs of sunspot activity at the Observatory of Zacatecas when he noticed strange objects crossing the face of the sun. In the two hours before clouds obscured his view he counted 283. The objects, traveling east to west, were apparently luminous. Bonilla succeeded in photographing some of the objects. These were probably the first UFO photographs ever taken, but like modern versions, they did nothing to help identify the objects. Other observatories are said to have seen the objects as well. This would indicate that they were outside the earth's atmosphere. When Camille Flammarion, renowned French astronomer, was shown the photographs he tentatively suggested that they were insects, birds, or dust.

The 19th century began with an impressive sighting at Baton Rouge, Louisiana. On the night of April 5, 1800, an object described as "the size of a large house" passed about 200 yards above the ground. It was brightly lit, caused heat to be felt on the ground, and took 15 minutes to disappear to the northeast.

The English astronomer Edmund Halley was sent a UFO report by an Italian professor of mathematics. He reported seeing in March 1676 a "vast body apparently bigger than the moon," which crossed over all Italy. It was at an estimated height of 40 miles, made a hissing sound and a noise "like the rattling of a great cart over stones." The professor calculated its speed at 160 miles a minute—9600 miles per hour. Halley's comment was: "I find it one of the hardest things to account for, that I have ever yet met." The next year, in 1677, Halley himself reported observing "a great light in the sky all over southern England, many miles high."

A number of years later in 1716 Halley saw a UFO that illuminated the sky for more than two hours. He could read a printed text in the light of this object. After two hours the brightness of the object was reactivated "as if new fuel had been cast in a fire."

In 1561 many people in Nürnberg reported seeing blood-red, bluish, or black balls and circular disks in the neighborhood of the rising sun. They were visible for an hour, and then appeared to fall to the ground as if on fire.

Even Christopher Columbus saw a UFO. He was patrolling the deck of the Santa Maria at about 10 p.m. on October 11, 1492 when he saw "a light glimmering at a great distance." He summoned another member of the expedition who also saw the light. It vanished and reappeared several times.

Some of these UFOs may well be accounted for by normal

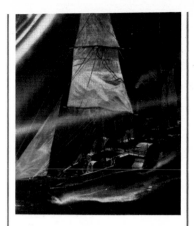

The Shining Wheel in the Sky

As a British steamer plowed its way through the Persian Gulf near Oman in the summer of 1906, an enormous wheel of light appeared. The vast wheel, seemingly bigger than the ship itself, was revolving in the sky not far above the surface of the water at that point. Vivid shafts of light emitted from the huge wheel and passed right through the steamer. But these beams fortunately did not interfere with the functioning of the boat in any way.

Since 1760 seamen have recounted sightings of unidentified flying objects in the form of a wheel. The Persian Gulf sighting of 1906 was one of eleven recorded reports between 1848 and 1910. Like most of the sea accounts of mysterious luminous wheels, this one remarked on the eery silence of the phenomenon. Also in common with most other such reports, nothing was said about humans or humanlike beings in the wheels, even though the ascent and descent of these objects were obviously controlled.

Were such glowing wheels in the sky an early and less sophisticated form of flying saucer? Were they operated by beings from other planets who kept themselves hidden or were invisible? Were they just visions of mariners too long at sea? No one has found an answer.

events. Others would probably stand up to rigorous study by today's scientists and join the large number of unsolved riddles on record. A few—like the aerial craft reported to have hovered over Bristol, England around 1270—would be too fantastic to study. The craft caught an anchor in a church steeple, and an occupant scampered down a ladder to free it. He was stoned to death by the crowd, which, regarding him as a demon, burned his body.

The story is reminiscent of an old Irish legend of which there are a number of versions. According to one account, a marvel happened one Sunday while the people were at mass in the borough of Cloera. "It befell that an anchor was dropped from the sky, with a rope attached to it, and one of the flukes caught in the arch above the church door. The people rushed out of the church and saw in the sky a ship with men on board, floating before the anchor-cable, and they saw a man leap overboard and jump down to the anchor, as if to release it. He looked as if he were swimming in water. The folk rushed up and tried to seize him; but the priest forbade people to hold the man, for it might kill him, he said. The man was freed, and hurried up to the ship, where the crew cut the rope and the ship sailed away out of sight. But the anchor is in the church, and has been ever since, as a testimony."

An even more remarkable account of contact between earth people and space visitors is said to have taken place some time during the reign of Charlemagne, who lived from A.D. 742 to A.D. 814. According to the version published by Brinsley le Poer Trench in his book, *The Flying Saucer Story*, spacecraft took away some of Earth's inhabitants to show them something of the way of life of space people. But when they returned the populace were convinced that their fellow men were members of the space race, whom they regarded as sorcerers. They seized these people and tortured them, and put many to death. Le Poer Trench quotes this passage from the original:

"One day, among other instances, it chanced at Lyons that three men and a woman were seen descending from these aerial ships. The entire city gathered about them, crying out that they were magicians and were sent by Grimaldus, Duke of Beneventum, Charlemagne's enemy, to destroy the French harvests. In vain the four innocents sought to vindicate themselves by saying that they were their own countryfolk, and had been carried away a short time since by miraculous men who had shown them unheard of marvels, and had desired them to give an account of what they had seen."

These four were about to be thrown into a fire when they were saved by Agobard, Bishop of Lyons. He listened to the accusations and to the defense, and decided that the four had not fallen from the sky at all. They were set free.

The further back in time we go, the more astonishing are the stories that are uncovered. The ancient Indian Sanskrit texts tell of gods who fought in the sky on aircraft—*vimanas*—equipped with deadly weapons. Many scholars regard these accounts as no more than the vivid imaginings of simple people who wished to bestow upon their gods the greatest conceivable powers. However, modern writers have pointed to

Above: Brinsley le Poer Trench, now Lord Clancarty, who has been involved in UFO research for 30 years. He is president of Contact International and a vice-president of the British UFO Research Association. He is a firm believer that UFOs visit Earth from other planets.

Left: a 16th-century Persian manuscript showing the legendary Kai Ka'ns going up in a fantastic flying machine. It is powered by enticing tied-up eagles to reach for raw meat impaled at the top.

Below: an Indian manuscript illustration of flying deities. In it the gods are coming to observe the outcome of one of the battles of the mythical champion Rajah Karna, told in the *Mahabharata*. Von Däniken has cited the numerous references to flying gods and flying machines —*vimanas*—as evidence for his theories of visitors from space.

Above: a 16th-century painting of the *Adoration of the Magi*. The peculiar behavior of the star that moved before the Three Wise Men in guiding them to Bethlehem, and came "to rest over the place where the child was" has made ufologists speculate that the star was in fact a spacecraft. It has also been pointed out that the Three Wise Men themselves —being dark and foreign— bear a remarkable resemblance to the mysterious three men in black of recent UFO history.

some astonishing similarities between these stories and 20th-century inventions. The following is from Protap Chandra Roy's translation of the ancient Indian manuscript the *Drona Parva* which he did in 1889, and which is quoted in a book by Desmond Leslie and George Adamski called *Flying Saucers Have Landed*:

"A blazing missile possessed of the radiance of smokeless fire was discharged. A thick gloom suddenly encompassed the hosts. All points of the compass were suddenly enveloped in darkness. Evil-bearing winds began to blow. Clouds roared into the higher air, showing blood. The very elements seemed confused. The sun appeared to spin round. The world, scorched by the heat of that weapon, seemed to be in a fever. Elephants, scorched by the energy of that weapon, ran in terror, seeking protection from its terrible force. The very water being heated, the creatures who live in the water seemed to burn. The enemy fell like trees that are burned down in a raging fire . . . The steeds and the chariots, burned by the energy of that weapon, resembled the stumps of trees that have been consumed in a forest conflagration. Thousands of chariots fell down on all sides. Darkness then hid the entire army . . ."

The scripts tell of a number of deadly weapons, including *Indra's Dart*, which was operated by a circular reflecting mechanism. It did not fire weapons, but was switched on like a searchlight. The shaft of light that was produced was aimed at a target which it was able to consume with its power.

These descriptions could easily be applied to nuclear bombs and laser beam weapons. Who were the possessors of such inventions, and what were the aircraft in which they traveled? W. Raymond Drake, in his book *Gods and Spacemen in the Ancient East*, quotes from a Sanskrit text which explains "the art of manufacturing various types of Aeroplanes of smooth and comfortable travel in the sky, as a unifying force for the Universe, contributive to the well-being of mankind." It gives a definition of a vimana as "that which can go by its own force like a bird, on earth, or water, or in air." Today, that which can travel in the sky from place to place, land to land, or globe to globe, is called "vimana" by scientists in aeronautics.

Some of the contents of the manuscript are listed as: "The secret of constructing aeroplanes, which will not break, which cannot be cut, will not catch fire, and cannot be destroyed. The secret of making planes motionless. The secret of making planes invisible. The secret of hearing conversations and other sounds in enemy planes. The secret of receiving photographs of the interior of enemy planes. The secret of ascertaining the direction of enemy planes' approach. The secret of making persons in enemy planes lose consciousness. The secret of destroying enemy planes . . .

"Metals suitable for aeroplanes, light and heat-absorbing, are of 16 kinds . . . Great sages have declared that these 16 metals alone are the best for aeroplane construction."

This translation, done by Maharishi Bharadwaja, is called *Aeronautics* and is described as *A Manuscript from the Prehistoric Past*. It is published by the International Academy of Sanskrit Research, Mysore, India. The unresolved question is:

74

Are scripts like these—possibly as old as the Old Testament—the work of inspired science fiction writers of their day, or are they eyewitness accounts of incredible events?

Perhaps further research will throw light on these perplexing questions. In the meantime, the UFO has enabled imaginative writers to reassess well-known past events in a new light. The Bible has proved to be a rich source of material. The star of Bethlehem that guided the Three Wise Men to the birthplace of Jesus is regarded by some ufologists as a flying saucer. They point to the fact that the wise men followed it until it "came to rest over the place where the child was." If it had been a bright star or planet, it would not have stopped at any point. But an unidentified flying object might well have hovered above one place. A writer who has explored UFO links in the Bible is Barry L. Downing, pastor of Northminster Presbyterian Church in Endwell, New York. He concludes that the miracles of the Old and New Testaments, usually ascribed to supernatural forces, could as reasonably be given an extraterrestrial interpretation. Instead of being spirits or messengers of God, angels could have been space visitors. God, reported to have spoken, could have been a being from another planet endeavoring to guide Earth people during crises.

Examining *Exodus* he points out that when the Israelites fled from Egypt, the Lord is said to have led them "by day in a pillar of cloud . . . and by night in a pillar of fire to give them light that they might travel by day and night . . ." This pillar, says Downing, was a flying saucer. Later, during their years in the wilderness, according to Downing it is a UFO that is referred to variously as the "Lord," "the angel of God," and a

Above: Moses receiving the Ten Commandments on Mount Sinai. B. L. Downing, a pastor of New York, considers that the "thick cloud" into which Moses vanished must have been a heavenly UFO. Below: a painting of *Moses and the Burning Bush*. Downing believes that the bush was burning because a flame-belching UFO had set down in the middle of it.

The book of Ezekiel in the Old Testament contains the prophet's description of his vision. It is open to many interpretations, but was long accepted purely as the mystical experience of a visionary. Today, however, some commentators explain it in terms of 20th-century technology. These three illustrations show different interpretations of the biblical prophet's strange vision.

Left: a traditional representation. It shows a conventional chariot with four wheels, and four winged creatures having the faces of a man, a lion, an ox, and an eagle exactly as described by Ezekiel.

"cloud." Certain verses in *Exodus*, says Downing, clearly show that Moses was in contact with space visitors who gave him the Ten Commandments, for example: "Then Moses went up on the mountain, and the cloud covered the mountain. The glory of the Lord settled on Mount Sinai, and the cloud covered it six days; and on the seventh day he called to Moses out of the midst of the cloud. Now the appearance of the glory of the Lord was like a devouring fire on the top of the mountain in the sight of the people of Israel. And Moses entered the cloud." Downing concludes: "Moses seems to have gone aboard the UFO, at which time he received stone tablets from the being in the UFO."

Most Christians will be excused for preferring a more orthodox, or even supernatural view of religious happenings. Few scholars would accept Downing's theories either. Like others before him with a new interpretation of our past, he tends to overstate his case to be persuasive, and risks losing credibility. But there are others who believe the Bible contains important UFO material, viewed from a scientific rather than a religious viewpoint. The Biblical account that has attracted the greatest attention among such believers is the striking experience of the Old Testament prophet Ezekiel.

The Book of *Ezekiel* begins with the remarkable vision that has caused so much excitement among modern ufologists. It is helpful to know the essential ingredients of Ezekiel's story before looking at the modern interpretation. It says: "Now it came to pass in the thirtieth year, in the fourth month, in the fifth day of the month, as I was among the captives by the river of Chebar, that the heavens opened and I saw visions of God . . . And I looked, and, behold, a whirlwind came out of the north, a great cloud, and a fire infolding itself, and a brightness was about it . . . And out of the midst thereof came the likeness of

Below: another view of the vision of the prophet. This artist has painstakingly worked out a literal interpretation of the account on the basis that it was miraculous and showed the power of the Lord.

four living creatures. And this was their appearance; they had the likeness of a man. And every one had four faces, and every one had four wings. And their feet were straight feet; and the sole of their feet were like the sole of a calf's foot; and they sparkled like the color of burnished brass. And they had the hands of a man under their wings on their four sides . . . Their wings were joined one to another; they turned not when they went; they went every one straight forward . . . two wings of every one were joined one to another, and two covered their bodies . . ."

Ezekiel goes on to describe how each of the four "living creatures" had an identical shining wheel that accompanied them even when they rose from the ground. Two things were strange about the wheels. They were constructed as though one wheel was inside another, and they could move in any direction without turning. Ezekiel gives many other details of his experience that has usually been regarded as visionary—simply as another attempt to describe mystical experiences in a way that others can understand. But it is different from other biblical visions because Ezekiel, a priest, goes into surprising detail. Whatever his belief about the Lord and angels, Ezekiel appears to have experienced something so totally alien to his knowledge and understanding that he sets out to give as much detail about the *construction* of what he saw as possible. Believers in flying saucers were quick to interpret his vision as a description of a spaceship and its occupants. Their explanation, however, left as many unanswered questions as the belief that Ezekiel's experience was purely mystical.

Erich von Däniken is among the writers who have postulated an extraterrestrial explanation of Ezekiel's vision. When Josef F. Blumrich, who had spent the greater part of his life on the

Below: this interpretation of Ezekiel's vision is based on present-day knowledge of space travel and astronauts. It was painted by a British aeronautical artist and pilot, Keith Mosely, who felt that von Däniken's theory was worth some thought. The four faces depicted literally in the first interpretation are in this case shown as three big insignia on the arms and chest of an extraterrestrial being, plus his own face. The machine that is propelled by rotor blades and has a base like a wheel carries the space visitors to the ground from their hovering mother ship. This fits in with Ezekiel's description of the men having wings, and of "a wheel upon the earth beside the living creatures, one for each four of them."

Above: Josef F. Blumrich, a NASA space engineer who spent most of his life designing and building aircraft and rockets—among them the giant Saturn V rocket. He became fascinated with von Däniken's view of the vision of Ezekiel as a visit of a UFO, and plunged into research to refute him. Instead he found that he himself became a convert. He worked out a reconstruction of the spacecraft he thought Ezekiel had witnessed, including details of how it might have been operated.

design and analysis of aircraft and rockets, read the suggestion he set about disproving it. After painstaking research, Blumrich decided that Ezekiel did see a spaceship. What is more he has produced detailed drawings of its construction, based on the prophet's description, which he says is a little ahead of our present technology. He gives the full details in his book, *The Spaceships of Ezekiel*. "Seldom has a total defeat been so rewarding, so fascinating, and so delightful!" he declared.

Blumrich, chief of the systems layout branch of the National Aeronautical and Space Administration (NASA), has worked on spaceship construction since he went to the United States from his native Austria in 1959. He is cobuilder of the Saturn V, and holder of many patents. In fact, Blumrich had been involved in designing and testing the wheel mechanism so accurately described by Ezekiel. This made him realize that the Bible texts could be describing a technical device rather than an ethereal vision. His further investigation led him to conclude that Ezekiel must have possessed extraordinary gifts of observation and an almost photographic memory. "This made it possible not only to develop a simple sketch, but also to express dimensions, weights, and capabilities in figures."

The four living creatures described by the prophet were not living at all, says Blumrich. They were the four legs of the huge spaceship, each with a wheel that could move forward and backward or revolve sideways. Such a wheel is now technically feasible and patented. Their wings were rotor blades. The geometry of these helicopter units made it appear that they touched each other when they rotated. The main propulsion system was by rocket engine, with the propellant stored in the huge top-shaped central body. The helicopter blades would have been used only for final touchdown maneuvers.

Blumrich believes that the results of his research "show us a space vehicle which beyond any doubt is not only technically feasible but in fact is very well designed to fulfill its functions and purpose. We are surprised to discover a technology that is in no way fantastic but even in its extreme aspects, lies almost within reach of our own capabilities of today, and which is therefore only slightly advanced beyond the present state of our technology. Moreover, the results indicate a spaceship operating with a mother spacecraft orbiting the earth.

"What remains fantastic is that such a spacecraft was a tangible reality more than 2500 years ago!"

The NASA scientist points out that later in his account the prophet describes being lifted and taken away by the spirit. This, he suggests, is further evidence that the vision was a spacecraft that transported Ezekiel to various places during the four times he met the extraterrestrial visitors.

Even though some puzzling biblical texts have provided the basis for the design of a space vehicle technically superior to our present designs, Blumrich's argument does not provide the indisputable proof required to convince the world that visitors from outer space have been in touch with mankind at points during its evolution. But a glance back through a few thousand years of our history is enough to show that UFOs—whatever they may be—are not a 20th-century phenomenon.

Blumrich's version of what Ezekiel may have been trying to describe. Left: the spacecraft as it would appear upon entering the earth's atmosphere. The four "men" that Ezekiel thought he saw were, says Blumrich, really four legs of the spaceship, which act as a kind of helicopter. During entry into the atmosphere, they fold back over the top of the spaceship, so making the braking potential fully effective. This phase of the flight would have been completed at the edge of the atmosphere, before Ezekiel saw the spacecraft.

Below: the landed spacecraft standing on the four helicopter legs. The brief bursts of the control rockets as the craft searched for a suitable landing space were interpreted by Ezekiel as lightning, and he saw the radiator of the reactor glowing like burning coals.

The First of the Contacts

For many people mysterious craft flying around overhead are one thing; tales of encounters with intelligent life commanding those craft are something else again. Yet many of those who claim to have been contacted by visitors from space tell their experiences with passionate sincerity. Right: one of the creatures that Betty and Barney Hill said had taken them aboard a spacecraft for what seemed to be a scientific examination. The Hills underwent hypnosis to recall the experience. Below: one of the goblins from a UFO that besieged the home of the Sutton family of Hopkinsville, Kentucky, for a harrowing night.

The meeting in the California desert between George Adamski and a man with long blond hair deserves to go into the history books as one of the most extraordinary events ever reported. If Adamski was telling the truth, his encounter near Desert Center in 1952 was a turning point in our history: the moment when an inhabitant of Earth came face to face with a visitor from Venus. If it was a hoax, it was one of the most elaborate and successful ever staged. As a result of it Adamski, an amateur astronomer, was able to travel widely and lecture about his contacts with extraterrestrials, and was feted by royalty.

"He suddenly saw the figure of a man... some way away..."

The modern flying saucer era was just over five years old at the time Adamski claimed he met a Venusian. Many people had become convinced that the flying saucers were interplanetary space vehicles, but the absence of any apparent attempt to contact the Earth's inhabitants was puzzling. Rumors of tiny creatures who had been taken from the scene of UFO crashes—dead or alive—were rife. Official secrecy was always given as the reason for absence of detail in such cases.

George Adamski, a 61-year-old Polish-born American, lived in the shadow of the famous Mt. Palomar Hale Observatory in California. He not only believed that UFOs were real, but he also felt sure that whoever was piloting them were humanlike beings. He and a group of fellow believers had been told of a number of flying saucer incidents in the area in which the objects were seen to descend close to the ground and even to land. The Adamski group decided not only to try to get good close-up photographs of the saucers but also to try to contact their occupants.

It was with this object in mind that Adamski and six others went into the California desert on November 20, 1952. Adamski felt he was somehow being guided by the space visitors, and the others allowed him to lead the way. They drove to Desert Center and then for another 10 miles in the direction of Parker, Arizona. Soon after stopping on the roadside to eat, the saucer hunters were rewarded by the sight of a large cigar-shaped UFO that had also attracted the attention of military planes in the area.

Adamski, a nondriver, shouted: "Someone take me down the road—quick! That ship has come looking for me and I don't want to keep them waiting! Maybe the saucer is already up there somewhere—afraid to come down here where too many people would see them." Two of the party drove off with him at once.

The group of saucer enthusiasts had already decided on the basis of personal observations that the cigar-shaped UFOs were mother ships: huge carriers that acted as bases for the smaller disk-shaped saucers. They did not, therefore, expect the object they were watching to make a landing, and when Adamski reached a desired spot between half-a-mile and a mile from the picnic area, he and the others in the car were not surprised to see the cigar-shaped UFO disappear over the nearby mountains. Adamski implored his two friends to leave him with his six-inch telescope, tripod and photographic equipment, and they went back to the rest of the party.

Within minutes his attention was attracted by a flash in the sky, and he saw a small craft that seemed to drift toward him. It settled itself in a cove about half-a-mile away. Adamski immediately found the flying saucer in the telescope and began taking photographs through a camera attachment. After taking several photographs Adamski removed the camera and placed it in its box. He then took out a Kodak Brownie in order to try a long shot. As he did so a couple of planes roared overhead and the saucer dropped down out of sight. He assumed it had returned to its mother ship, but after a few minutes he suddenly saw the figure of a man standing at the entrance of a ravine some way away. The man beckoned to him. Puzzled, Adamski decided that someone needed help, and he set off in that direction.

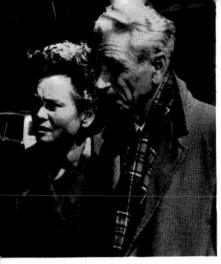

Left: George Adamski on a lecture tour in Europe in 1959, pictured with the secretary of the Dutch UFO Contact Group. In 1952 Adamski had claimed that he had met and talked with Venusians. Below: Adamski's snapshot of the object he said was a Venusian scout ship in takeoff (arrowed). This was his first meeting with Venusians on November 20, 1952. It was witnessed by a group of six of his friends who were interested in investigating UFOs.

Left: a Venusian's footprint that Adamski claims was deliberately left by the space visitors. There were three sets of deep and distinct prints, and Adamski believed they had been made with special shoes designed to leave a special message for the people on Earth. Right: sketches of the patterns found on the Venusian footprints made by Betty Bailey, one of the witnesses. Adamski and his friends spent a great deal of effort and time trying to read the symbols, which they felt contained vital information for those on Earth.

Left footprint

Right footprint

As he got closer Adamski noticed that the figure was slightly smaller and younger than he was, and dressed in ski-type trousers. His long hair reached to his shoulders, which was most unusual for a man at that time.

"Suddenly, as though a veil was removed from my mind," Adamski wrote later, "the feeling of caution left me so completely that I was no longer aware of my friends or whether they were observing me as they had been told to do. By this time we were quite close. He took four steps toward me, bringing us within arm's length of each other.

"Now, for the first time I fully realized that I was in the presence of a man from space—*a human being from another world!*"

Adamski estimated the man's age as about 28, his height as 5 feet 6 inches, and his weight around 135 pounds.

"He was round-faced with an extremely high forehead; large, but calm, gray-green eyes, slightly aslant at the outer corners; with slightly higher cheekbones than an Occidental, but not so high as an Indian or an Oriental; a finely chiseled nose, not conspicuously large; and an average size mouth with beautiful white teeth that shone when he smiled or spoke."

Conversation was difficult, for the spaceman did not appear to speak much English and Adamski did not recognize the man's language. Instead, they communicated by a combination of telepathy and sign language. In this way Adamski established that the man came from Venus, that the space visitors were concerned about bombs and radiations emanating from the Earth, and that they operated their craft by the law of attraction and repulsion. During this discussion the Venusian pointed to his flying saucer, which was hovering above the ground unnoticed by Adamski. When it was time for him to depart the man from Venus walked over to his spacecraft with Adamski. He indicated that the Earthman should not get too close, but Adamski forgot and moved underneath the outer flange of the hovering saucer. "My arm was jerked up, and almost at the same instant thrown down against my body," he said. "The force was so strong that, although I could still move the arm, I had no feeling in it as I stepped clear of the ship."

The Venusian assured Adamski that feeling would return to his arm, which it did after some weeks. What concerned Adamski more was that the seven exposed photographic plates in his right pocket may have been affected by the strange power. He put his hand in his pocket and removed them. The Venusian indicated that he would like to take one. He made it clear that he intended to return it at a future date.

The time had now arrived for the brief meeting between two civilizations to end, and the Venusian bade his Earth companion farewell. He stepped onto a bank behind the saucer, from there onto its flange, and entered his spacecraft without Adamski seeing how he did so. In moments the flying saucer, looking like a heavy glass bell, rose up and moved off into space.

What made Adamski's account seem plausible to many people was that his six friends had witnessed the encounter from a distance. His book *Flying Saucers Have Landed*, which was co-authored with the British writer Desmond Leslie, contains

Left: a sketch of the Venusian made by Alice Wells who watched the meeting through binoculars. Adamski remarked that the sketch "conveys the broad features of his appearance but is far short of doing him justice." Mrs. Wells was one of the witnesses who signed a notarized statement.

Below: an artist's conception of the meeting of Adamski and the Venusian in the California desert.

photographs of their testimonies, signed before notaries public. They said:

"We, the undersigned, do solemnly state that we have read the account herein of the personal contact between George Adamski and a man from another world, brought here in his Flying Saucer "Scout" ship. And that we were a party to, and witnesses to the event as herein recounted."

The declarations were signed by Mr. and Mrs. Al C. Bailey of Winslow, Arizona; Dr. & Mrs. George Hunt Williamson of Prescott, Arizona; Mrs. Alice K. Wells, owner of Palomar Gardens and operator of the café there; and Mrs. Lucy McKinnis, Adamski's secretary.

They had not been able to hear the conversation, of course, but they had seen the small domed saucer, and had watched Adamski speaking to a man in a one-piece suit. Mrs. Wells even drew a picture of the Venusian after looking at him through binoculars.

Before he left the space visitor drew Adamski's attention to the footprints he had left in the sand. He was wearing shoes decorated with an inscription on the soles, designed, it seems, to leave a message for the world. Williamson took a number of plaster casts of the footprints immediately after the strange desert encounter. He has since written a number of books on flying saucers which include a detailed analysis of what these inscriptions may represent.

On December 13, 1952 the Venusian scout ship visited Adamski again. This time there was no contact, but as it swooped low over Palomar a porthole window opened and Adamski's photographic plate was thrown out. A hand waved and the craft sped away, but not before Adamski had taken a number of pictures through his telescope. These showed the craft in great detail, and established the Adamski saucers as the classic shape in the mind of the public. His is an upturned saucer with three balls underneath, appearing to be landing gear. On top is a circular cabin with portholes. Many other observers have claimed to have seen similar flying saucers and to have photographed them, but the Adamski pictures were the most influential and

Left: the photograph that Adamski said had been substituted for one of his by the Venusians. They had borrowed one of his photographic plates on their first meeting with him, and returned it on December 13 by dropping it from their scout ship near the spot he had set up his telescope. The original subject had been washed off. Adamski said the substitute picture was of writing from another planet. Below: a telescopic picture of the underside of the Venusian spacecraft, taken by Adamski as it dropped off the photograph.

widely accepted among those who believed in UFO contacts.

Adamski's later encounters with his friends from other worlds were even more fantastic. In his second book *Inside the Space Ships*, Adamski claimed, following a hunch, he went to Los Angeles and he booked into his favorite hotel. There he was approached by two men who greeted him with a special handshake identifying them as space dwellers. They looked like ordinary people, had on normal clothes and wore their hair short, and spoke with hardly a trace of an accent. They drove him out of the city for a rendezvous with the scout ship. He learned during this journey that one of his companions was from Mars, the other from Saturn. When they reached the flying saucer Adamski was delighted to find his Venusian friend. This time, for some inexplicable reason, he spoke perfect English.

The men from the three planets took him aboard the craft and for a ride in the flying saucer. Adamski gave them names to help identify them in his narrative, although he said they did not use names as we do. The Venusian he called Orthon, the Martian Firkon, and the Saturnian Ramu.

A lens in the floor of the saucer enabled Adamski to view the earth as the scout ship climbed into space. It went aboard the mother ship where Adamski was greeted by other extra-terrestrials including two extremely beautiful women pilots who kissed his cheek. It was during this space trip that Adamski was told the reason for the coming of the saucers. It was to warn "of the grave danger which threatens men of Earth today" through atomic explosions. There was also a danger that atomic explosions on earth could upset the balance of the galaxy and the lives of others on neighboring planets.

During another space flight with his friendly planetary contacts—whose ages ranged from 40 to several hundred years—Adamski claims he was taken to view the moon. His space friends told him that earth scientists were wrong about the satellite. Its conditions were not as extreme as imagined.

"There is a beautiful strip or section around the center of the moon in which vegetation, trees, and animals thrive, and in which people live in comfort. Even you of Earth could live on that part of the moon, for the human body is the most adaptable machine in the Universe."

On the side facing the earth, vegetation was sparse but Adamski saw a small furry four-legged animal running about. Later, when he was taken to the other side of the moon, Adamski claims he saw cities, mountains, rivers, and lakes. "Actually, we seemed to be drifting over the rooftops, and I could see people walking along clean, narrow streets." Adamski was also shown live pictures from Venus, beamed onto an invisible screen. These too showed cities and earthlike scenery. He noticed that animal life was similar to ours, and he saw birds like canaries as well as horses and cows.

George Adamski died on April 23, 1965, four years before our first landing on the moon. He did not live to see space exploration shatter the illusions of his numerous followers. We now know with certainty that there is no life on the moon, and that Venus and the other planets in our solar system are unlikely to support

Below: a diagram of a Venusian scout ship, based on Adamski's description after he had taken a trip with three extraterrestrials. One of them was his old acquaintance from the first contact.

VENUSIAN SCOUT SHIP

ILLUSTRATED BY
GLENN PASSMORE

A sequence of photographs taken by Adamski on March 5, 1951. Left: one of the Venusian scout ships has been launched and a second one is just emerging from the long cigar-shaped mother ship.

Left: four of the scouts have appeared, still hovering close to the mother ship, and a fifth is being released from the bottom.

Below left: six scout ships and the mother ship in a cluster. All are enveloped in a bright glow.

Below: a photograph of Adamski (on the right) and a Venusian peering out of the portholes of a small mother ship. According to Adamski it was obligingly taken by another Venusian from a scout ship with Adamski's own Polaroid camera. Adamski made the common photographer's complaint that he could have used more film than he took with him.

intelligent life. Adamski, then, was either fooling us, being fooled by someone else, or having a psychological experience that he thought was real. He has also left us with at least one puzzle that keeps him from being entirely discredited.

In his account of his first alleged space flight he describes the experience in these words:

"Firkon motioned me to come to one of the portholes as he said, 'Perhaps you would like to see what space really looks like.'

"I soon forgot my disappointment as I looked out. I was amazed to see that the background of space is totally dark. Yet there were manifestations taking place all around us, as though billions upon billions of fireflies were flickering everywhere, moving in all directions, as fireflies do. However, these were of many colors, a gigantic celestial fireworks display that was beautiful to the point of being awesome."

Compare Adamski's words with those of astronaut John Glenn during the first manned orbital space flight:

"The biggest surprise of the flight occurred at dawn . . . When I glanced back through the window my initial reaction was that the spacecraft had tumbled and that I could see nothing but stars through the window. I realized, however, that I was still in the normal attitude. The spacecraft was surrounded by luminous particles. These particles were a light yellowish green color. It was as if the spacecraft were moving through a field of fireflies."

A coincidence? Adamski's account was first published in 1955. Glenn's flight was on February 20, 1962. Perhaps this can mean that Adamski had a genuine contact with extraterrestrials, but that his version of what happened was greatly embellished to make it acceptable to the general public.

Adamski never claimed that his experience was unique. The space people had told him that they were contacting others, he said. Naturally a whole crop of such stories soon appeared. Most offered nothing in the way of corroborative evidence, and each seemed to be vying with its predecessors to be more fantastic.

Serious UFO investigators, particularly those who believed the saucers were interplanetary, did not know which way to turn. Here was the evidence they had been waiting for, but now that

Below: a diagram of the mother ship showing the landing chute at the top and the launching chute at the bottom, as printed in the book *Flying Saucers Have Landed* by Adamski. On the left is the hangar deck where scout ships are stored when not in flight.

Above: a copy of the sketch made by the painter and writer R. L. Johannis of two UFO pilots he encountered in the hills of Italy in August 1947. This was one of the earliest contact stories to get international news coverage. Below: a drawing of the creature seen near a UFO in Flatwoods, West Virginia on September 12, 1952. It is held by one of the witnesses. The being had glowing greenish-orange eyes and seemed to be about 10-15 feet tall. It floated slowly toward a group of observers who panicked and fled. Some were violently ill later.

it had arrived they did not want it. They believed that these stories of personal contact with space people would do more harm to the cause of serious research than a thousand denials by military authorities. Some UFO enthusiasts abandoned their interest; others went back to studying obscure objects and lights in the skies while studiously ignoring claims of contact; but some persevered. Trying to establish a pattern in the contact accounts was practically impossible. It seemed that if every account were true, they must each concern visitations from different planets. There were giants, dwarfs, hairy creatures, smooth-skinned humans, and numerous permutations.

The two earliest contact stories to come to light happened in the year flying saucers became hot news, just 29 days after Kenneth Arnold made his famous sighting on June 24, 1947 and five years before Adamski's story. José C. Higgins, a survey worker, was with a group of others in an isolated area of Brazil when a large circular craft of grayish white metal descended from the sky with a whistling sound. Higgins' companions ran away. The huge UFO—it was about 150 feet wide—settled on the ground on curved metallic legs, and three figures got out. It was not clear whether they were male or female. They were about 7 feet tall, and their heads and bodies were covered with inflated transparent suits. Underneath they seemed to be wearing clothes made of brightly colored paper. They wore metal boxes on their backs, and all had identical heads—large, round, and with big eyes. They had no eyebrows or beards. Higgins found them strangely beautiful. They drew eight circles on the ground, indicating that the seventh was their home. This was later interpreted as meaning that they came from Uranus, the seventh planet. Higgins eluded their efforts to entice him aboard the spaceship, and watched for half an hour while they jumped and leaped around, tossing enormous stones. They then climbed back into their vehicle and vanished into the sky.

A month later in Italy, Professor R. L. Johannis, a well-known painter and writer, encountered a very different kind of space visitor. On August 14, 1947 he was out searching for fossils near a small village in the northeast of Italy. Equipped with a knapsack and a geologist's pick, he was making his way along a valley when he saw a large red lens-shaped object embedded in the mountain rock in front of him. From it protruded two antenna. Not far away he saw what he thought were two boys, but as he neared them he realized to his horror that they were strange dwarves. They were only about 3 feet high and their heads gave the impression of being larger than a normal person's. They wore dark blue overalls of a translucent material with vivid red collars and belts. Brown caps covered any hair they may have had, and their skin was green. Their mouths were small slits like those of fish, and their eyes were round and protruding like large yellow-green plums. As they came closer the professor found that he was rooted to the spot, petrified. Eventually he raised his arm, pointed at the spacecraft, and shouted to find out who they were and whether he could help them.

The dwarves seem to have mistaken his action as being hostile, and he was suddenly hit by a ray emitted from the belt of one of the creatures, knocked to the ground, and almost paralyzed.

Above: laughing dwarves from outer space. In 1954 they were said
to have popped out of a spool-shaped flying saucer and accosted
an Italian woman in the woods. They snatched one of her stockings
and the carnations she was carrying. Then they disappeared.

They Talked Till Dawn

While asleep in his truck at midnight on July 28, 1952, Truman Bethurum of Prescott, Arizona was awakened by strange visitors – short spacemen in coveralls. They took him to their spaceship and he talked to their beautiful female chief till dawn. Then he wrote this note, as printed in *Life* magazine in 1957: "To whom it may concern. If I am found dead it will be because my heart has stopped from the terrible excitement induced by seeing and going aboard a flying saucer."

Spaceship Inspection

One night in the summer of 1953 George Van Tassel lay sleeping in the desert near Giant Rock. To his surprise a spaceman woke him and offered to let him inspect a spaceship nearby. Van Tassel said yes and, clad only in shorts, was lifted straight up in an upright position. He had a good look at the spaceship, and was impressed by inventions that included a closet which cleaned clothes automatically with light. After a thorough inspection, Van Tassel left on a gravity nullifying beam.

It Rained Space People

Ruth May Weber of Yucca Valley, California had a psychic experience involving space people. She was told by a voice that Earth was already inhabited by space people, who would take over in case of a world disaster. This voice message was confirmed when she saw a shower of spacemen and women raining from the skies on Main Street in the town. They disappeared into the crowd entirely unnoticed by the ordinary Yucca Valley residents, who went on about their ordinary business.

The dwarves came toward him, and one of them bent down to retrieve the pick he had dropped. Horrified, the professor saw that he had jointless green claws instead of hands. The two dwarves climbed back into the disk embedded in the rock, and in a few moments it shot out of the cleft. For a while it hovered over the terrified man. Then it shot away. It took Professor Johannis a long time to muster enough strength to get up from the ground. When he had partly recovered he noticed that his thermos was shattered, and that there was no trace of the metal container. An aluminum can and fork had disappeared, and so had his geologist's pick.

The year of 1952 in which Adamski claims first to have met space visitors was a vintage one for contacts. Mayor Oskar Linke reported that he and his daughter Gabrielle were four miles inside the Soviet zone of Germany on their way back to the Western zone when they came across two humanlike figures dressed in one-piece silvery suits. One had a flashing light on his chest. Nearby, resting in the forest glade, was a saucer, 50 feet wide and shaped like a large oval warming pan. When these beings heard the voices of Herr Linke and his daughter they immediately ran to their craft, which took off amid roars and flames. They watched as it whistled away over the treetops.

Next came Orfeo Angelucci whose alleged communications with the occupants of the saucers was on a telepathic level. He claimed to have seen a red light in the sky release two green disks. When these came to rest a few feet from his car a voice spoke in English. Then a screen appeared between the two UFOs, and the faces of a most noble man and woman appeared. His discourse lasted two hours. During another encounter he was taken aboard a saucer and given a ride.

Not all the reported contacts were so friendly. On September 12, 1952 a group of youngsters reported seeing a meteor land on a hill at Flatwoods, West Virginia. On the way to investigate they stopped at the home of Mrs. Kathleen Hill. She, her two sons, and a 17-year-old National Guardsman, Gene Lemon, decided to join the search. As they climbed the hill they saw a large globe which one said was "as big as a house." One boy heard a throbbing sound, another a hissing noise. The group's attention was suddenly drawn to a huge figure concealed in the branches of a tree. It was between 10 and 15 feet tall and had a blood-red face and glowing greenish orange eyes. When this monster floated toward them they fled hysterically down the hillside. Some of the group were violently ill for the rest of the night. The following day parallel skid marks were found on the grass, and a strange smell lingered over the ground.

This is one of the few contact stories involving a monster. Humanlike operators are far more common, though their appearance covers a wide range from the terrible dwarves seen by Professor Johannis to the beautiful female pilot whom Truman Bethurum, a mechanic, encountered in the Nevada desert. Her name was Captain Aura Rhanes, and she spoke English in rhyming couplets. She told him she came from a world behind the moon, the planet Clarion. Captain Rhanes was $4\frac{1}{2}$ feet tall, wore a black skirt, red blouse, and a beret. Her crew consisted of 32 men, all small like herself. After 11 meetings the

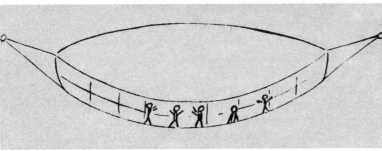

Left: Betty and Barney Hill. They sighted a UFO and subsequently discovered they had lost track of two hours and 35 miles of distance. During hypnosis to help Barney Hill overcome anxiety, the missing two hours were accounted for. The couple had been on a spacecraft whose crew examined them like laboratory animals, and released them with the promise that they would remember nothing.

Left: Barney Hill's sketch of the UFO as it looked when they first saw it traveling parallel with their car on an empty road.

space visitors were apparently frightened off by Bethurum's familiarity with them in a restaurant. He approached the captain and eight of her crew in the restaurant saying: "Ma'am, we have met before? Say, ain't these the little guys from Clarion?" They all got up, walked to the exit, and vanished into thin air!

In February 1954 an English writer of thrillers, Cedric Allingham, claimed to have met a man from Mars at a lonely spot in Scotland. He said he had seen and photographed a flying saucer while out bird watching, and had continued walking along the coast after lunch. The saucer flew in from the sea, and he was able to photograph it as it came to rest 50 yards away. It was similar to Adamski's saucers with its three-ball landing equipment. A humanlike being with a very large forehead stepped out. A small tube was attached to his nose, presumably as an aid to breathing on Earth. He communicated by drawing in the writer's notebook. Topics touched on were the atom bomb, the Martian canals, and the shortage of water on Mars.

While those who claimed contact with space people were entertaining the public and making a good living out of it, there was a steady build-up of saucer activity that involved UFO landings and takeoffs without contact. Jacques Vallee, French-born astronomer, expert on computer techniques, and consultant to NASA on the Mars Map project, contributed to the book *The Humanoids* a report of 200 such sightings during 1954 alone. On November 8 of that year, for example, a man saw a light in a stadium in Monza, Italy and soon a crowd of 150 people gathered. They destroyed the barriers and rushed in to have a look. They saw a craft on three legs emitting a blinding white light. Figures in light colors and transparent helmets were seen standing close by. One had a dark face and a trunk or hose coming up to his face. They seemed to communicate with guttural sounds. The strange disk flew away without any noise.

A year later the Sutton family of Hopkinsville, Kentucky, were besieged by little monsters from a saucer. A visiting relative on his way home reported seeing a UFO land in a nearby field. Minutes later the family saw a small glowing figure approaching the house. It was no taller than $3\frac{1}{2}$ feet, had a roundish head, elephantine ears, a slit mouth from ear to ear, and huge wide-set eyes. It appeared to have no neck, and its long arms ended in clawed hands. It dropped to all fours when it ran. Several of these creatures roamed around the outside of the Suttons' lonely home, climbing trees and clambering onto the roof. A gun was fired through a screen door at one of the figures. It was knocked over by the blast but ran away. After a night of terror, the family scrambled into a car and drove into town to report their experience.

In England in 1957, a Birmingham housewife claimed to have been visited by a spaceman in her own home. He did not arrive in a flying saucer, nor would the neighbors have seen him at the door. He simply materialized, accompanied by a whistling sound, in the living room of 27-year-old Mrs. Cynthia Appleton. He was tall and fair and wore a tight fitting plasticlike garment. He communicated by telepathy and produced TV-like pictures to illustrate his flying saucer and a larger master craft. He indicated

Above: one of the occupants of the UFO that the Hills sighted. The information for the picture was given under hypnosis more than two years after the event. Until the deep trance therapeutic sessions, the Hills had no conscious memory of the experience.

Left: an artist's impression of the UFO crew members Betty and Barney Hill described as their abductors. They had two slits where nostrils would be, but no nose, and their mouth had no muscle. Their eyes were elongated and seemed to give a wider field of vision than we have. All wore dark clothing that looked alike.

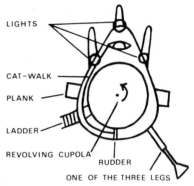

LIGHTS

LIGHTS

CAT-WALK

PLANK

LADDER

REVOLVING CUPOLA

RUDDER

ONE OF THE THREE LEGS

Above: two drawings by Antonio Villas Boas of the UFO on which he had a trying experience. He was plowing a field alone when he was kidnapped by the crew.

Above: Antonio Villas Boas, a young Brazilian farmer, undergoing a medical examination after his strange encounter with the crew of a UFO. In 1957 he claimed to have had a passionate sexual experience with a beautiful tiny space woman, after he had had a blood sample taken from his chin. The doctor found that Villas Boas had been subjected to radiation, and that there were two unexplained needle marks on his chin.

to her that he came from a place of harmony and peace. At the end of this and other visits he simply dematerialized.

The missing two hours in the lives of Betty and Barney Hill after a UFO sighting are regarded by many as the final proof that flying saucers are spaceships from other worlds. The couple was returning to their New Hampshire home on September 19, 1961 after a short vacation in Canada. During their journey they spotted a light in the sky that grew larger and appeared to be following a parallel course to their car. Then they saw a UFO a few hundred feet ahead of them. They stopped their car, and Barney viewed the huge structure through his binoculars. He saw two rows of windows from which figures peered out at him. He ran back to the car and drove off. They heard a beeping sound and felt drowsy. Two hours later they heard the noise again, and slowly became aware that they were driving 35 miles south of where they had seen the object. They could not account for their activities during the lost period. A compass reading showed that their car appeared to have been subjected to radiation.

They immediately reported their sighting to Pease Air Force Base and to the National Investigations Committee on Aerial Phenomena (NICAP), a UFO research group in Washington DC. It was not until three years later, when Hill was extremely sick and undergoing psychiatric treatment, that hypnosis revealed what seemed to have happened during the missing two hours. Both Betty and Barney Hill underwent hypnotic regression to uncover the experience, and their accounts agreed.

According to both of them, after hearing the odd beeping they were taken from their car by a strange group of men and carried onto a huge spacecraft. Separately they were laid on operating tables and carefully examined. He felt someone putting a cup over his groin. She had a large needle inserted into her navel. Samples of hair and toenails were taken. The spaceship's occupants were puzzled that his teeth came out whereas hers did not. The Hills were told that they would not remember their ordeal when released.

An even more bizarre abduction occurred in Brazil on October 15, 1957. Antonio Villas Boas, a 23-year-old farmer, had twice sighted bright unidentified flying objects. One day after the second sighting while ploughing a field, he claimed that a huge egg-shaped luminous object appeared and landed in front of his tractor. Terrified, he leaped off and ran away only to be grabbed by the arms, lifted from the ground, and carried into the saucer by three figures in tight gray overalls and helmets. There were other occupants on board the saucer, and they all communicated with strange sounds resembling barks or yelps. Villas Boas was stripped naked and sponged all over. A blood sample was taken from his chin. Then he was left alone in a room with a couch. After a while a naked woman entered the room. She was about 4 foot 5 inches tall, and had the most beautiful body he had ever seen. Her hair was almost white, her eyes were large, blue, and slanted. She had high cheekbones, a straight nose, and a pointed chin. She moved toward him and embraced him. The result of this strange meeting between inhabitants of two worlds was a passionate sexual encounter. It was not all bliss, however. Villas Boas recounted that "some of the grunts that I heard coming from that woman's mouth at certain moments nearly spoiled everything, giving the disagreeable impression that I was with an animal."

The Villas Boas account is perhaps the ultimate in saucer contact stories. It may well have been discarded as the sexual fantasy of a young man were it not for the medical examination he underwent soon after reporting the encounter. Dr. Olavo T. Fontes reported that the farmer had been subjected to sufficient radiation to produce symptoms of radiation poisoning over a long period. At the point where blood was said to have been taken from his chin the doctor found two small hypochromatic patches. The skin looked smoother and thinner, as though it had been renewed.

If just a few of the contact stories are true, then we on Earth may be under close scrutiny by creatures from outer space. If the Villas Boas story is also genuine, then somewhere out in space a remarkable breeding experiment may now be in progress.

Yamski or Adamski?

E. A. Bryant, a retired prison officer who lived in southwest England near Dartmoor prison, was taking a walk on the evening of April 24, 1965. About 5:30 p.m. he arrived and stopped at an especially scenic spot. All at once he saw a flying saucer appear out of thin air about 40 yards away. It swung left and right like a clock pendulum before coming to rest and hovering above ground.

Although he was frightened, Bryant was curious enough to overcome his fears and stay to watch. An opening appeared in the side of the spaceship and three figures, dressed in what looked like diving suits, came to it. One beckoned to Bryant, and he approached the strange craft. As he did so, the occupants removed their headgear. He saw that two had fair hair, blue eyes, and exceptionally high foreheads. The third—who was smaller and darker—had ordinary earthly features.

The dark one talked to Bryant in fairly good English. Bryant understood him to say his name was "Yamski" or something like it, and that he wished "Des" or "Les" were there to see him because the latter would understand everything. He also said that he and the others were from the planet Venus. After the UFO took off, some metallic fragments were left on the ground near the place it had been. Later some small pieces of metal were indeed found there.

When Bryant reported his experience, investigators were struck by the fact that George Adamski, author of the best-selling book *Flying Saucers Have Landed*, had died the very day before. His collaborator on this book had been Desmond Leslie. Was there a connection between "Yamski" and Adamski, and "Des" or "Les" and Desmond Leslie?

The Aliens Are Among Us!

As interest in flying saucers increased in the 1950s, some UFO enthusiasts began to seriously consider an extraordinary idea. Perhaps they should look for evidence of extraterrestrial visitors on the surface of this planet rather than in the skies. It might be that beings from outer space had already infiltrated our communities and were living among us, gathering information and making contact with those who were sympathetic to the possibilities of life in other worlds. This theory had already gained currency in the strange accounts of those who had claimed contact, called contactees in UFO jargon. Adamski and others, having first

Above: is this woman a visitor from outer space? Her name is Marla Menger, and her husband Howard claims that she is an extraterrestrial being with whom he has been in contact since he was only ten years old.

Right: a science fiction comic-book cover. At first most of the speculation about the occupants of flying saucers ran along the lines of little green men. When the idea of space visitors that look just like us presented itself, the possibilities for contact were excitingly wide-open.

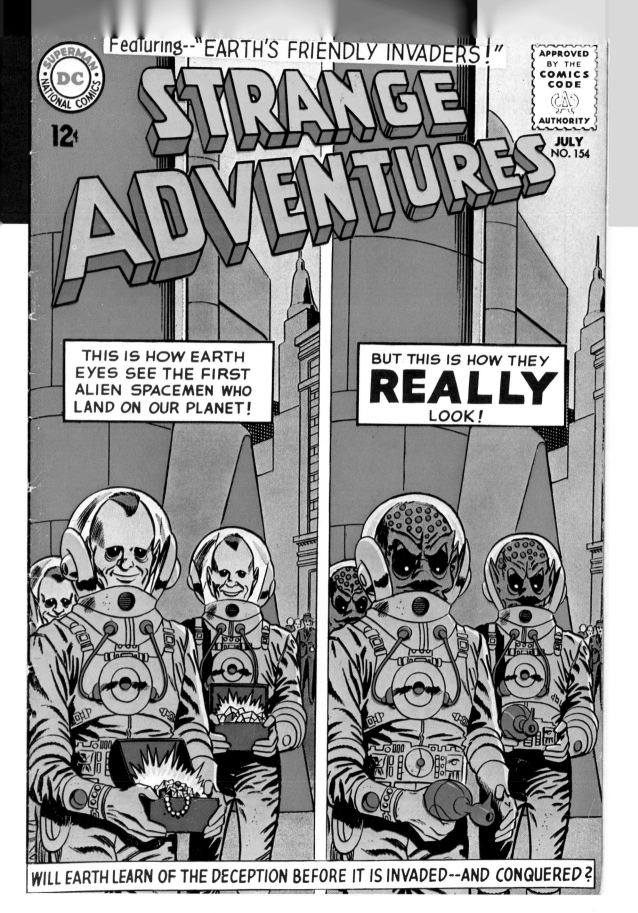

"A UFO landed ... two men and a beautiful girl stepped out."

met the space people dressed in space clothes and close to their spaceships, later claimed to have met them dressed as we do, and frequenting hotels and restaurants. This belief made the need for supporting evidence in the way of photographs unnecessary. Anyone could claim to have met someone from space in their homes or on the streets.

One of the most famous contactees of this period was a New Jersey signpainter, Howard Menger, who had apparently been meeting space people from an early age. But it was in his army days during World War II, when a long-haired blond man in a car contacted him, that he realized their true identity. Some time later, a UFO landed near his parents' home in June 1946, and two men and a beautiful girl dressed in pastel "ski uniforms" stepped out. The space woman, who said she was 500 years old, told him to learn to use his mental powers so as to be ready for important events in the future. She said he should not talk about his experiences until 1957. It was in that year, during a rash of UFO sightings in High Bridge, New Jersey where he lived, that several witnesses claimed they had watched as Menger went out to speak with the space people. The full story was related in Menger's book *From Outer Space to You*. It was even more bizarre than Adamski's account, and told of his many contacts with space people posing as ordinary Earth people such as businessmen and real estate dealers.

During an early radio broadcast about his alleged contacts, Menger met a striking blonde girl named Marla who was one of a crowd that had gathered outside the studio. He later divorced his wife and married Marla who, he claimed, was from another planet. The next fascinating twist to the story came when Marla wrote a book entitled *My Saturnian Lover*. The Saturnian in question was Menger! His space visitors had told him that he was originally from Saturn. This was divulged during one of his many conversations with them, for they frequently dropped in for coffee at his home. During these visits he was also asked to cut their long golden tresses to make them look more like earthly inhabitants. He was taken for a flight to the moon from which he brought back some strange rocks. He said they were moon potatoes.

While many contactees painted a cosy picture of their encounters with the people of the UFOs, there was another more sinister aspect. This came to the public's attention in 1953 when the International Flying Saucer Bureau, a fast-growing saucer society in the United States, suddenly closed down. Albert K. Bender had started the organization in January 1952. It was nonprofit and soon attracted members and officers eager to solve the UFO mystery. But Bender found himself caught up in a series of events that terrified him. They culminated in his decision to close the IFSB less than two years later. In the last issue of the bureau's journal *Space Review*, the following statement appeared:

"The mystery of the flying saucers is no longer a mystery. The source is already known, but any information about this is being withheld by orders from a higher source. We would like to print the full story in *Space Review*, but because of the nature of the information we are sorry that we have been advised in the negative." The statement went on to tell the journal readers:

"We advise those engaged in saucer work to please be very cautious."

All that was known by most of Bender's UFO associates was that he claimed to have been visited by three men in black. Some believed he was perpetrating a gigantic hoax in order to gain personal publicity. Others believed he had hit on the right solution to the UFO puzzle and that the government, knowing this, had silenced him. He lost friends, and some of his closest saucer colleagues were openly hostile. Bender refused to reveal "the truth" until 1962. But when he told it in his book *Flying Saucers And The Three Men*, he was subjected to even greater derision. It read like the most incredible science fiction.

Bender claimed that soon after the Bureau opened he began to experience strange phenomena, including a telepathic phone warning that he should not investigate saucers any more. This was followed by the appearance of a glowing object in his room. The glow left a pungent smell of sulphur which was to become a regular feature of the manifestations. When at the movies once, he became aware of a man seated next to him with "two strange eyes, like little flashlight bulbs lighted up on a dark face." This figure disappeared, reappearing instantly in a seat on the other side of the saucer researcher. Thoroughly rattled, Bender called the manager; but by the time he had arrived with his flashlight the mysterious figure was nowhere to be seen.

Some months later, Bender went upstairs to his room after a meeting, and noticed that someone had opened his door. A strange blue light emanated from within. As he entered, armed with a broom, he saw that the glow came from one corner. Some object seemed to be in the center of the light. Bender shouted, "Cut the kidding and come out of there!" and the glow began to fade, leaving the image of two glowing eyes for several minutes.

Above left: Howard Menger, the New Jersey signpainter whose alleged contacts with the world of Venusians, Saturnians, and other inhabitants of our solar system were wild and wonderful.

Above: Menger's trip to Venus. His first wife was a simple Earthling and he had to creep out of bed in the middle of the night to keep his rendezvous with spacecraft awaiting him in Field Location No. 2, on a farm. This artist's impression shows him viewing the wonders of Venus on a wide screen in a spacecraft that is passing over the planet. Menger's second wife Marla, who was said to be an extraterrestrial, confused things by claiming that he was not an Earth man either. She wrote about his true identity in her book *My Saturnian Lover*.

Then the room was normal except for a strong smell of sulphur everywhere.

March 15, 1953, was the day chosen by the International Flying Saucer Bureau to send a telepathic message to occupants of flying saucers, asking them to make contact and help the world solve its problems. A time was appointed, and each member of the IFSB was asked to repeat mentally an identical message. Bender lay down on his bed to carry out his part of the program. As he repeated the message for the third time he felt the most agonizing pain in his head. He could smell a strange smell like burning sulphur, and small lights began to swim through his brain. He felt ice cold. As he opened his eyes he seemed to be floating above his bed. It was as if his soul had left his body and was looking down on it. Suddenly a voice seemed to come from in front of him. It was as though it permeated him without issuing an audible sound. He was warned not to delve any further into the mysteries of the Universe. He was told that "they" had a special assignment "and must not be disturbed by your people." When he tried to remonstrate the voice added: "We are among you and know your every move, so please be advised we are here on your Earth."

A few days later the mysterious communicators made an appearance to Bender. As with many other visits, their arrival caused the saucer researcher to suffer pain and discomfort. In his book he wrote:

"Blue lights appeared from nowhere and swirled about in the room. I grew dizzy as the areas above my eyes throbbed and

Above: Menger and several other contactees from all over the earth, were given a Moon tour. This is one of the pictures he snapped as a souvenir of the trip, of which he wrote regretfully that he was not allowed to photograph any surface detail, people, or mechanical installations. In his picture, according to Menger's account, a Venusian is shown standing in front of his spacecraft after it has landed on the Moon's surface.

Above: on the Moon. The round object is the Moon base, and a Venusian spacecraft is flying in the emptiness above it.
Below: two photos of Menger's "free energy motor," which he constructed one evening in his signpainting shop apparently under telepathic control. It was a kind of perpetual motion machine. The first and most successful version crashed through the roof and he was unable to duplicate it.

again felt puffy. I stumbled to the bed and threw myself upon it. As I did so, I felt my body growing icy cold. I could feel I had quickly come under the complete power of someone or something.

"The room seemed to grow dark yet I could still see. I noted three shadowy figures in the room. They floated about a foot off the floor. My temples throbbed and my body grew light. I had the feeling of being washed clean. The three figures became clearer. They looked like clergymen, but wore hats similar to Homburg style. The faces were not clearly discernible, for the hats partly hid and shaded them. . . . The eyes of all three figures suddenly lit up like flashlight bulbs, and all these were focused upon me."

By telepathy the three visitors gave Bender a message. He was told that the UFOs had a purpose in visiting Earth, and that they must not be disturbed until their goal was accomplished. "As you see us here, we are not in our natural form. We have found it necessary to take on the look of your people while we are here." Bender was told that they had made numerous contacts with Earth with their spacecraft, and they had established a base at a remote spot on this planet. He had been selected as a contact because he was so ordinary. This meant no one would believe him if he betrayed their secret.

"We also found it necessary to carry off Earth people to use their bodies to disguise our own," Bender was told. They gave him a small disk, about the size of a coin. He was told to grasp it in his hand, turn on his radio, and repeat the word "Kazik" three times if he should wish to contact them.

Left: Albert K. Bender, a UFO investigator and founder of a successful civilian sighting group, the International Flying Saucer Bureau. He became the center of curiosity and controversy when he abruptly closed the Bureau in 1953, saying only that he had done so after a visit from three mysterious men dressed in black. He refused to say anything more at all about it for seven years.

Right: Bender's sketch of one of the three men in black who so ominously materialized in his room. They were in disguise.

Above: the proposed cover of a magazine for saucer enthusiasts designed by Bender. Although he did not explain it at the time, in 1953, it shows how his visitors survived on their home planet. Avoiding the barren surface, they lived underground and used crater openings as launching pads for their spacecraft, as shown. When these were not in use, the planet would appear to be dead.

At this point most serious UFO researchers reading Bender's account doubtless decided that their former colleague had taken leave of his senses. But the one-time head of the civilian saucer investigation group had even more incredible material to relate. During his next contact with the three men in black he was somehow transported by them to a huge circular room with a glass dome, bathed in a brilliant glow. It may have been the interior of a flying saucer. He was greeted by a man who revealed that the purpose of the UFOs was to take a valuable chemical from our seas. To carry out their purpose, they had their people placed in strategic places everywhere including the Pentagon. They could destroy the world with a flick of a switch. Bender was shown various scenes on a three-dimensional screen, including one of a hideous monster. It was, he wrote, "more horrifying than any I have ever seen depicted in the work of science fiction or fantasy artists. The monster was alive." Without Bender noticing it, the speaker disappeared. Suddenly his voice came from the image of the monster, and he told Bender that that was his normal appearance, and they all looked like this on their home planet although they, of course, found nothing strange in their own appearance. He was told that there were three sexes on his planet: male, female, and a third of neither sex who were the exalted ones—the leaders. The females laid eggs that were stored and hatched as necessary. The planet from which they had traveled was many many light years away.

During another contact with this strange space race, Bender claims to have been taken to see their base of operation in the Antarctic, to have examined a flying saucer at close quarters, to have seen a flying saucer garage, and finally to have come face to face with an exalted one—a 9 foot bisexual with the same shining eyes as the others. This creature told Bender they had been visiting Earth since 1945 and would stay for about 15 years. "We have carried off many of your people to our own planet for means of experimentation, and also to place some of them on exhibit for our own people to see," this base commander told the saucer researcher. He warned that Bender would be taken if he got in their way. Back on Earth, Bender's eerie adventure continued. An invisible entity, whom Bender spotted only by the indentations on an armchair, visited his room. When the invisible form materialized Bender experienced "the worst fright of my entire life." He saw a 10-foot tall creature, greenish all over except for a glowing red face and glowing eyes. Bender fainted.

The space people's intrusions into Bender's life were not without compensations. On another visit to the bright glass dome, he was stripped by three beautiful women dressed in tight white uniforms. He was placed on an operating table and the three women applied a liquid and "massaged every part of my body without exception, turning me over on my stomach and my sides. They expressed no emotion, neither that of revulsion nor enjoyment, as they carried out the matter."

An object was lowered over his body and he was bathed in a light that changed from lavender to deep purple. Afterward he was told that this was to ensure that he would enjoy good health for years to come. At the same time he was subjected to a ray that created an impulse in his body which their instruments could detect at all times. "We have found it necessary to do this in order to keep you under our constant surveillance. If at any time you reveal our secret we need only press a button in our laboratory and your body will be destroyed. It will disintegrate and very little will be left of it." That was the penalty for divulging his knowledge.

With that threat over him, and knowing "the secret of the saucers," Bender decided to wind up his organization. He was told that he was to keep the strange disk hidden. When it disappeared, he would know that the space visitors had accomplished their mission, and he could then discuss his contacts with them. According to Bender, the departure took place in 1960. He went to his strongbox where he kept the disk, having smelled the strange odor of sulphur. He threw open the lid and saw that it had disappeared. What is more, all his other possessions in that box had turned to dust.

He decided to write about the encounters although he knew, as he states in the book, that almost no one would believe him. But he claimed that "since the metal disk vanished and the visitors from space left our planet, flying saucer reports have decreased."

There is certainly no more reason for accepting Bender's incredible tale than that of other contactees. But there is one factor that has caused many investigators to ponder a little before dismissing it as horrific science fiction. That is the role of the three men in black. These mysterious men have cropped up time and again in the flying saucer riddle. In the early days it was assumed that they were government or CIA personnel, either taking a keen interest in the activities of certain UFO researchers or groups, or actively attempting to censor news of UFOs. Time and again the three men in black were reported to have called on UFO witnesses or researchers. They arrived in shiny black Cadillacs and were invariably described as small dark-skinned Orientals. They carried official looking cards or passes, and

The "Exalted One" From Outer Space

UFO enthusiasts were startled when the International Flying Saucer Bureau stopped all activity in late 1953. Although less than two years old, the organization founded by Albert K. Bender in Bridgeport, Connecticut had been prospering. Why did it shut down?

The only person who could answer this question was Bender himself, and he was not talking. Not until seven years later did he talk—and his tale was one of contact with an "Exalted One" from space.

Bender claimed to have had a direct interview with the Exalted One, who warned him of instant death if he continued to delve into the mystery of UFOs. That's why he disbanded the IFSB. But he learned many interesting things during his interview, and he revealed all when he got the sign he could.

In his interview, for example, Bender asked the space being if his people believed in God. The reply was that they did not, because they did not have the desire to "worship something" as Earth people do.

Another topic Bender discussed with the space visitor was whether other planets were inhabited. The Exalted One said that there had once been life on Mars, but that it was destroyed by invaders. The Martians had built beautiful cities and developed a vast system of waterways, but had not been as technologically advanced at the time of their end as we now are. Venus was developing life, the being said.

One of the most interesting exchanges between Bender and the Exalted One was about the moon. Bender asked if the Earth people would ever reach the moon, and he was told yes.

Seven years after Bender wrote this, men were indeed walking on the moon.

Above: Rex Heflin, who managed to get four Polaroid pictures of a UFO he sighted in 1965. All four originals disappeared after he gave them to some mysterious callers who claimed that they were official investigators, but who were unknown to the agencies they said they represented.
Below: William Hartmann, professor and investigator on the Condon Committee, working on the Heflin saucer sighting.

appeared to have a great knowledge of UFO phenomena. It was not until the late 1950s that some of the flying saucer authors began checking on the three men in black. They discovered that if they gave their identities, these proved to be false. Occasionally someone tried to follow one of the Cadillacs, only to lose it, often in circumstances which indicated that it had vanished or dematerialized. Though they usually turned up in threes, the men in black occasionally worked alone or in pairs. Typical of these reports is one cited by the Colorado Report, which had been carried out by the University of Colorado with the backing of the United States Air Force.

Case Number 52, occupying 18 pages of the massive report, deals with a series of UFO photographs taken by Rex Heflin, a California highway inspector. He sighted a metallic disk in the sky above Santa Ana Freeway and took three Polaroid photographs of it and one of a smoke ring the UFO is alleged to have left behind when it flew away. The case received widespread publicity, and he was interviewed by civilian UFO investigators as well as Air Force personnel. The El Toro Marine Air Station took a special interest in the case. Among his many callers Heflin received a man claiming to be from the North American Air Defense Command (NORAD), and he gave him the originals of the photographs. These were never returned and NORAD subsequently denied that any of its representatives had visited the UFO witness. The sighting was on August 3, 1965. Fortunately Heflin had copied the original photographs, but the mystery of his sighting and the visitor remained unsolved. Strangely, when the Colorado team began investigating the Heflin case as part of its independent assessment of the flying saucer situation, the highway inspector received another mystery caller. This is how the Colorado report deals with the incident:

"According to the witness, on 11 October 1967, during the period when our investigation was beginning, an officer in Air Force uniform came to the witness's home in the evening and presented his credentials. Mindful of past experience, the witness studied them carefully. They gave the name Capt. C. H. Edmonds, of Space Systems Division, Systems Command. . . . The man allegedly asked a number of questions, including 'Are you going to try to get the originals back?' The witness claims that the man appeared visibly relieved when the witness replied 'No.' The officer also assertedly asked what the witness knew about the 'Bermuda Triangle' (an area where a number of ships and aircraft have been lost since 1800s).

"This alleged encounter took place at dusk on the front porch. During the questioning, the witness says he noted a car parked in the streets with indistinct lettering on the front door. In the back seat could be seen a figure and a violet (not blue) glow, which the witness attributed to instrument dials. He believed he was being photographed and recorded."

When the Colorado investigators followed up this lead they discovered that of the four "C. H. Edmonds" on the Air Force's list of officers, there was none with the corresponding rank and spelling. "All were of rather high rank and none should have had any connection with the Santa Ana case."

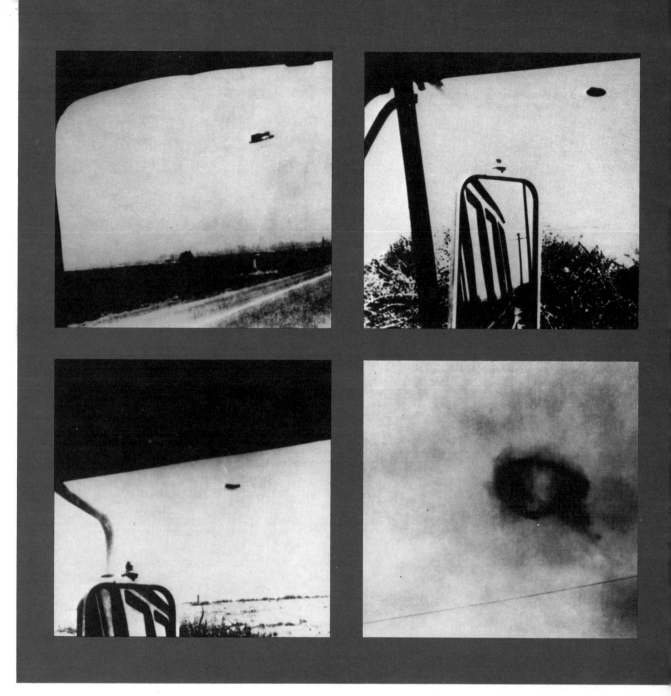

Afterward Heflin told investigators he believed his phone was being tapped and his mail intercepted. He also said that on three or four occasions his neighbors had told him that men in military uniform had come to his door during the day when he was not there.

Another case involving apparent imposters in uniform was investigated by writer John Keel in his book *Operation Trojan Horse*. In November 1966 two women had been watching flashing lights in the night sky in Owatonna, Minnesota, when one of the lights moved rapidly toward them, and then hovered a few feet above the ground at the far end of the field in which they were standing. One of the witnesses fell to her knees in a trancelike state. The other, Mrs. Ralph Butler, was astonished to hear a strange metallic-sounding voice emanating from her

Above: the photographs that Heflin took through his truck window. The fourth shows the smoke ring that the UFO left as it vanished. Hartmann discovered that by hanging a Leica lens cap just a few inches outside the window, a picture very similar to the second photo could be achieved.

Right: two investigators of UFO phenomena in Germany hold the corpse of a creature said to be a dead crew member of a flying saucer. The UFO from which the body came had crashed near Mexico City in the 1950s, and the bodies found in it were sent to Germany for thorough study.

Below: the spirit photography of the 19th century takes a modern swing in the 20th— a lawyer from the west of England took a picture of his young daughter and was astonished to discover the image of a "spaceman" behind her when the photograph was developed.

friend's lips. "What . . . is . . . your . . . time . . . cycle?" it asked. Mrs. Butler tried to give an answer explaining how the year was divided into days and hours and so on, and after several more questions the friend suddenly returned to normal and the object shot away. They were excited about the experience, but discovered that when they tried to discuss it with others they were both plagued with blinding headaches.

After reading one of Keel's UFO articles in a magazine Mrs. Butler wrote to him about their experience, and he phoned her. During an hour-long discussion she suddenly asked: "Has anyone ever reported receiving visits from peculiar Air Force officers?" The journalist said he had heard a few such stories, and she went on to give the following account:

"Well, last May (1967) a man came by here. He said he was Major Richard French, and he was interested in CB [citizen's band radio] and in UFOs. He was about 5 feet 9 inches tall with a kind of olive complexion and pointed face. His hair was dark and very long—too long for an Air Force officer, we thought. He spoke perfect English. He was well educated."

He wore a gray suit, white shirt, and black tie, and everything he was wearing was brand-new, she said. He drove a white Mustang whose license number her husband noted, and later found out it was a rented car from Minneapolis. The man said his stomach was bothering him and she advised him to eat jello. She said that if it continued to bother him he could come back for some, which he did the following morning. Mrs. Butler sat him at her kitchen table and produced a big bowl of jello. To her surprise he picked the bowl up and tried to drink it. "I had to show him how to eat it with a spoon," she told Keel. Later the same man turned up in Forest City, Iowa, and visited some of the Butlers' close friends.

Research has shown that there was a Richard French in the Air Force in Minnesota, but he did not even remotely answer to the description of the mysterious "major" who called on Mrs. Butler.

It has not escaped the attention of some UFO researchers that many of the humanoid figures reported near landed flying saucers are of similar build to the men in black and have the same facial characteristics. Their skin is described as olive-colored or tanned, their eyes are said to be large but with an Eastern cast or slanted, and their faces are sometimes described as pointed. As far back as the 1897 aircraft sightings in the United States, a certain Judge Lawrence A. Byrne came across a strange looking object anchored to the ground. "It was manned by three men who spoke a foreign language," he told the *Daily Texarkanian*, "but judging from their looks, would take them to be Japs. They saw my astonishment and beckoned me to follow them, and on complying I was shown through the ship."

Not having been able to solve the saucer riddle, some of the researchers have concentrated their studies—and their imaginations—on the pursuit of the men in black. They have come up with some surprising conclusions. The men in black appear to have a mission, not always sinister. Their role might appear to be one of guiding the human race, or at least endeavoring to influence the course of its history. Some claim that they tried and succeeded when they brought to the attention of King Herod's court the imminent birth of Christ. The three wise men with Oriental features and dark skin who "came from the East" were the men in black—or the biblical equivalent. Not only did they show the same preknowledge of events that their modern equivalents demonstrate, but they even led the way to Bethlehem. They never returned to King Herod, as they had promised, but "went home by another way."

The Bible is almost as rich in stories of the three men—usually regarded by scholars as angels—as it is in alleged UFO accounts. In Genesis there is a description of three men who appeared before Abraham and ate and drank with him.

Other Bible accounts bring to mind once more the frightening encounters that saucer researcher Albert Bender claimed to have had with the men with shining eyes. Enoch, we are told, dreamed of two very tall men "such as I have never seen on earth. And their faces shone like the sun, and their eyes were like burning lamps. . . . They stood at the head of my bed and called me by my name. I awoke from my sleep and saw clearly these men standing in front of me." This might be regarded as just a coincidence, but the story continues with a familiar theme. The men took him into the sky on a tour of "seven heavens." On his return to Earth he wrote an account of his experiences which is *The Book of the Secrets of Enoch.*

Supporting evidence is to be found in The Book of *Daniel.* The famous prophet saw "wheels as burning fire" and a figure that came down from a "throne" in the sky. The being's hair was like

Below: Lonnie Zamora, a New Mexico patrolman who chased a speeder and was distracted by a descending UFO throwing out a flame. He found it landed in a gully, with two aliens in light clothing. He took cover, and the craft took off again. When another policeman came along to help Zamora, who was rattled, he verified the presence of landing marks and smoldering plants where the UFO had set down.

pure wool. It was dressed in a white robe with a gold belt, and it had a luminous face and two glowing eyes.

"And I Daniel alone saw the vision: For the men that were with me saw not the vision; but a great quaking fell upon them so that they fled to hide themselves.

"Yet I heard the voice of his words; and when I heard the voice of his words, then was I in a deep sleep on my face, and my face toward the ground."

Some might argue that Bender had read these biblical stories and based his own shining-eyed visitors on the descriptions of Enoch and Daniel. But that does not explain the many similar creatures seen by UFO witnesses.

On October 9, 1954, for example, a French farmer riding his bike near Vienne, France, saw a figure dressed in a diving suit. It had boots without heels "and *very bright eyes.*" Two headlights were placed one above the other on its very hairy chest. It disappeared into the forest. Nine days later in Fontenay-Torcy, France, a man and his wife saw a red-colored cigar-shaped object in the sky. It dived toward them and landed behind some bushes. Suddenly the couple was confronted by a bulky individual just over 3 feet high whose eyes *gleamed* with an orange light. One of the witnesses lost consciousness.

On the beach at Ain-el-Turck near Oran, Algeria, a small man *with glowing eyes* was seen six days later. The following month, on November 28, two truck drivers in Venezuela found the road blocked between Caracas and Petare by a luminous sphere about eight to 10 feet wide, hovering about six feet above the ground. One got out of the truck and was approached by a small bristly dwarflike creature with claws and *glowing eyes.* A tussle took place and the driver was thrown 15 feet. He drew a knife to protect himself but found that stabs had no effect on the dwarf. The other driver ran for the police. Two similar creatures appeared from the bushes, apparently carrying stones and earth samples. They rushed into the sphere, and one of them blinded the embattled driver with a light to enable the third creature to flee. The sphere took off.

These incidents, all occurring in the space of a few months, do not prove Bender's story, of course; but they do illustrate that glowing eyes are a feature of some UFO accounts. We have also seen that similar beings appear to have been encountered during biblical times. The really sinister aspect of Bender's story is his assertion that these space visitors can take the form of humans, or even possess the bodies of abducted humans, in order to live on this planet. In fact, almost every contactee has claimed that the visitors from outer space, whatever their real guise, are living ordinary lives on Earth as part of an infiltration plan.

If the space people's purpose is simply to prepare the human race for ultimate contact with a superior space civilization, we have nothing to fear. But some UFO writers are worried. They point out that the men in black have mysteriously appeared in cases that can have nothing to do with such an ultimate goal. Amateur sleuths investigating President John Kennedy's assassination, for example, have come across these enigmatic individuals. The American writer John Keel comments in his book *Our Haunted*

Above: an artist's impression of the UFO that reportedly landed in the yard of Joe Simonton's Wisconsin chicken farm in 1961. In it were three small dark men, one of whom asked Simonton for water. As he gave them a pitcher of water he saw that they seemed to be cooking, and asked for a sample of the foodstuff. It appeared to be a perforated cookie. The man gave him four, and then the UFO whizzed out of sight. Left: Joe Simonton with one of the peculiar cookies he got from the UFO crew. Analysis showed that they were made of corn and wheat flours, but the origin of that type of wheat was unknown.

Planet: "Here the black Cadillacs and the slight, dark men in black suits are viewed as Cubans and CIA agents. Paranoia runs high because now over 50 witnesses, reporters, and assassination investigators have met with sudden death, some under the most suspicious circumstances. The full story of Kennedy's murder in Dallas in 1963 is filled with incredible details, many of them similar to things found in the most mysterious of the UFO incidents. Photos and physical evidence have vanished or been tampered with just as in so many UFO cases."

Probably there is no link. Probably the men in black had no involvement in the assassination of the president. But strange coincidences bedevil the history of flying saucer research, leading investigators along new and bizarre paths and producing more and more fantastic theories to solve the puzzle.

It is probably also just a coincidence that Dallas, Texas— scene of Kennedy's assassination—has been a favorite haunt of flying saucers since the early days of the UFO era.

7

UFOs Today

According to a Gallup poll of 1966, more than five million people in the United States claimed that they had actually seen a flying saucer, and about 50 million—nearly half the adult population—believed that unidentified flying objects were real. But the official attitude continued to be negative. In 1969 the Condon Committee, which with the backing of the Air Force had been studying the problem for several years, finally published its massive report. This concluded firmly that UFOs did not exist. On the basis of its recommendations the Air Force closed down Project Blue Book, its own official inquiry into flying saucers.

The United States Air Force has decided UFOs do not exist. Even newspapers have become somewhat jaded about UFO sightings. Still the sightings continue to be reported, many by people who are as baffled and as stubbornly insistent that they saw some kind of flying object as were the first UFO-sighters some 20 years ago. Right: this brightly colored UFO was sighted in France at about midnight on March 23, 1974.

"A brilliant egg – shaped object about 200 feet long..."

But the public, as ever, remained unimpressed by official pronouncements. Another Gallup poll taken in 1973 revealed not only that half the adult population in the United States still believed in UFOs, but also that by then more than 15 million claimed to have seen one, an increase of 200 percent in seven years.

Since the military has washed its hands of UFO investigations, the long-established civilian organizations like the National Investigations Committee on Aerial Phenomena (NICAP) and the Aerial Phenomena Research Organization (APRO) are steadily gaining in stature. Many scientists and other highly qualified investigators belong to these and other research groups both in the United States and other countries. Well-known figures in the world of astronomy—for example, Dr. J. Allen Hynek and Dr. Jacques Vallee—are conducting their own research projects. Their books have added a respectable image to the field of UFO literature, which has seen too many sensational publications for its own good. Their work is concerned with quality of sightings rather than quantity, and they look for patterns in the appearance and behavior of UFOs that will help them build up recognized types of objects. Once types have been established, they might be able to conjecture further about the composition and source of power of flying saucers.

Typical of the sightings that interest these researchers were the remarkable events around Levelland, Texas, on the night the Soviet Union launched its second satellite carrying a dog into orbit on November 2, 1957. It was at 11 p.m. that the police received the first report. A truck driver and his companion had encountered a brilliantly lit torpedo-shaped object about 200 feet long. It had passed low over their truck at a rapid speed, apparently causing the lights to go out and the engine to stop. The men were petrified. As the object moved away, the truck lights came on again and the engine started.

An hour later the police received a call from a man who had come across a brilliant egg-shaped object about 200 feet long. It was sitting in the road about four miles east of Levelland. As he approached his engine failed and his headlights went out. He was about to get out of his car when the object rose and disappeared. He then found that his engine and lights were working again. The next report was from a man who had also seen a bright object sitting in the road 11 miles north of Levelland. His engine also stopped and his lights went out, returning to normal as soon as the object flew away.

A freshman from Texas Technical College about nine miles east of the town had trouble with his car at about this time. The engine stopped and the lights went out. It was not until after he checked under the hood that he noticed an oval-shaped object, flat on the bottom, sitting on the road ahead. He estimated its length at about 125 feet, and said it appeared to be made of a metallic or aluminumlike material. It glowed blue-green. He was scared, but, unable to start his car he sat and watched it for several minutes. It soon rose vertically into the sky and disappeared "in a split instant."

As further reports came in the police decided to take a look

Below: Dr. J. Allen Hynek, an astronomical consultant to Project Blue Book, remains convinced that many sightings were explained away too lightly. He believes that a methodical correlation of the various sightings—however bizarre some seem— will help establish recognized types of sightings and show up any patterns that exist.

for themselves. Though none experienced close encounters or interference with their cars, two policemen reported seeing bright lights for just a few seconds. Levelland Fire Marshall Ray Jones was in the same area that night, and reported that his car headlights dimmed and his engine sputtered at the very moment he spotted "a streak of light" in the sky.

A total of 15 independent calls were received by the police that night. Every caller was excited. None of those who got close to the strange illuminated craft had any doubt about its existence. No satisfactory explanation has been offered for the Levelland episode, and since then the same interference with car engines, headlights, and radios has been reported on numerous other occasions.

The Levelland case is given in detail in *The UFO Experience* by J. Allen Hynek, former astronomical consultant to the Air Force's Project Blue Book. Dr. Hynek is an eminent astronomer. He is director of the Lindheimer Astronomical Research Center at Northwestern University and Chairman of the Northwestern Astronomy Department. He was for several years an associate director of the Smithsonian Astrophysical Observatory at Cambridge, Massachusetts, and headed its NASA-sponsored satellite tracking program. Since the early flying saucer days he had been employed as a scientific consultant on UFOs by the Air Force. As such he had been responsible for explaining many allegedly strange sightings as perfectly normal astronomical phenomena. But he also soon found that, though many sightings could be accounted for by misidentification of astronomical or other phenomena, there still remained some for which there was no easy explanation, and which were puzzling even to experts like himself. He became increasingly disenchanted with Project Blue Book's methods of working. The team was undermanned. Records were kept in chronological order with almost no cross-references. Worst of all, the investigators on the whole seemed more concerned with slapping a quick explanation on each sighting, rather than attempting to evaluate the problem in depth. The last straw for Hynek and those like him was the imbalanced Condon report that effectively caused the Air Force to abandon its investigation into UFOs.

Hynek likens the present situation on the UFO problem to that surrounding the meteorite debate nearly two centuries ago when meteorites were dismissed as "old wives' tales." Their existence was denied by science, and people who reported them were ridiculed and regarded either as mad, deluded, or hoaxers. We know now that those who saw meteorites were witnessing a real physical phenomenon. Stones did and do drop out of the sky, but Hynek does not know of any astronomer who had one land at his feet. In the same way, the evidence for UFOs depends largely on the accounts of eyewitnesses without scientific backgrounds, and there are still those scientists who adopt the attitude: "I won't believe it until I see it myself."

The problem is that UFO researchers can be just as biased in the other direction. Many adopt a theory about the flying saucers and then look for evidence to support it. Since UFO phenomena are so varied, it is not difficult to find several

Above: Jim Lorenzen, a civilian deeply interested in methodical UFO research. In 1952 he and his wife Coral, who is also heavily involved in collecting and collating UFO reports, founded the Aerial Phenomena Research Organization (APRO). It acts as a clearing house for reports.

sightings to demonstrate the truth of almost any theory. Such researchers carefully omit other sightings which do not fit their pet ideas. Investigators such as Dr. Hynek and Jacques Vallee, the well-known astrophysicist and mathematician, insist that all aspects of the strange phenomenon must be studied if we are to solve the UFO puzzle. Their books deal with analysis of types of UFOs—such as nocturnal lights and daylight disks— as well as types of encounters ranging from close proximity aerial sightings to landings of craft and crew. There are recognizable patterns into which UFOs fall, but there are many contradictions that cause continuing confusion in UFO circles. So while the scientists search for tangible physical proof, others have turned to the occult in an attempt to find explanations for many of the astonishing incidents surrounding UFO cases.

Typical of the incidents which have moved thinking toward the occult was Patrolman Herbert Schirmer's encounter with a UFO in Ashland, Nebraska in 1967. It was 2:30 a.m. on the morning of December 3. As 22-year-old Officer Schirmer was approaching an intersection on Highway 63, he saw an object ahead with a row of flickering lights. When he put on his main headlights, however, the object shot into the sky and disappeared. Half an hour later, back at the police station, his log book entry contained these words: "Saw a flying saucer at the junction of highways 6 and 63. Believe it or not."

Schirmer went home with a headache and a buzzing noise in his head which prevented him from sleeping. He also noticed a red welt that ran down the nerve cord of his neck below the left ear. It was not until Officer Schirmer was investigated by the Colorado team that he discovered he had apparently been contacted by the occupants of the UFO.

During time regression hypnosis his subconscious filled in the details of 20 missing minutes in his police report, immediately after seeing the UFO. He described following the object after it had landed in a field. He tried calling the police at Wahoo, Nebraska, to report the incident but his radio, lights, and engine were not working. The object, like a bright football, had three telescopic legs that descended as it settled on the ground. Then beings stepped out of the UFO shooting a greenish gas at him and his car. One of them pointed a bright ray that paralyzed him and caused him to pass out.

His next hypnotic memory was of being grabbed by the neck by one of the beings who had humanlike features. He was asked if he would shoot at a space ship. When he said he would not, Schirmer was told he could come aboard for a few minutes. The occupants were between $4\frac{1}{2}$-feet to 5-feet tall, and wore close-fitting silvery-gray uniforms and an antenna on their hoods or helmets. Their heads were thin and longer than human, with a flat nose, a slit for a mouth, and slightly slanted eyes that did not blink. They had a gray-white complexion. Schirmer, while still under hypnosis, was able to describe the inside of the flying saucer and its equipment. The occupants also projected pictures on a screen. Though the leader spoke to him, he was told his mind was also receiving simultaneous data input. Schirmer learned that they had come from a nearby galaxy. They had bases on Venus and other planets including Earth.

Right: meteors were once classed as superstitious nonsense by most scientists, as UFOs are now, and the people who reported seeing them were treated with the same condescending disbelief that meets many who claim to have sighted UFOs today. It is ironic that the Condon report suggests that many UFO sightings may in fact be sightings of meteorites. This painting of the 11th century shows a lumpy asteroid falling past an astounded observer.

Above: a group of the local villagers gather around a meteorite that fell to earth in Bacubirito, Mexico. The appearance of a meteor is as unpredictable as that of a UFO, so many photographs of such objects in flight have resulted when meteors crossed into the field of a camera that was being used to photograph something else entirely.

Below: a gigantic crater left by a meteorite near Winslow, Arizona.

Above: police officer Herbert Schirmer, sketching the UFO he saw while on duty in Nebraska. He said under hypnosis he had been taken aboard. He had no memory of the event before being put into a trance, having recalled only the blinking lights that had first attracted his attention. Below: Schirmer's drawing of the crew leader of the spacecraft.

On Earth their bases were underground or under the ocean.

"They have no pattern for contacting people," said Schirmer during the trance interrogation. "It is by pure chance so the government cannot determine any patterns about them. There will be a lot more contacts . . . to a certain extent they want to puzzle people."

After about 15 minutes inside the UFO, Schirmer was told not to reveal that he had been on board the craft. He was simply to report the first stage of his sighting. The beings appeared to have planted this hypnotic suggestion in his mind, for he had no conscious memory of his extraordinary experience although he did feel troubled and uneasy. It was only under hypnotism that the details came out. In this his experience was like that of Betty and Barney Hill in 1961, who only recalled a visit on board a spaceship under hypnosis several years later.

Six years after the Schirmer incident in October 1973, two shipyard workers encountered the occupants of a flying saucer in Pascagoula, Mississippi. It is one of the most celebrated contacts of the 1970s. Though they did not need hypnosis to remember what took place, they both separately underwent hypnotic-regression, and their stories under hypnosis tallied. They revealed the most amazing information.

Charlie Hickson and Calvin Parker were fishing on the west bank of the Pascagoula River at about 7 p.m. when they spotted a strange object, emitting a bluish haze, about two miles away. It came toward them to within about 30 yards, and hovered three or four feet above the river. Both men were petrified. Three occupants emerged and floated toward them. Parker, aged 19, got hysterical and passed out. Hickson, aged 42 and known for his calm and coolness, was rigid with fear. One of the creatures emitted a strange buzzing sound. The two others, who had pinchers instead of hands, lifted Hickson up under the arms and glided on board their craft with him. Their vehicle was oblong and about 8-feet high with an opening at one end. Outside it was lit by a strange blue light and inside it glowed brightly. The creatures placed Hickson in a horizontal position where he floated while they examined him with a large eyelike device. They left him alone for a while and then returned. He tried to talk to them but they took no notice of his questions. Hickson was too scared to get an accurate idea of what they looked like. They seemed to be about 5-feet tall, and to have something projecting where a human nose would have been. Beneath this projection was a slit, but it never seemed to move. The head apparently sat on the body without any neck. He had no remembrance of eyes or hair. When they finally let him go, the vehicle made a buzzing sound and disappeared.

The two men were interviewed by Sheriff Fred Diamond and Captain Glen Ryder at the Sheriff's office in Pascagoula four hours after their terrifying experience. Their testimony was tape recorded. Then, to see if the whole thing was a hoax, they were left alone and the tape recorder was left running without their knowledge. Hickson sounded shaky and Parker was frantic as he recalled how his arms could not move.

Parker: "I passed out. I expect I never passed out in my whole life."

Hickson: "I've never seen nothin' like that before in my life. You can't make people believe—"

Parker: "I don't want to keep sittin' here. I want to see a doctor—"

Hickson: "They better wake up and start believin' . . . they better start believin'. . . ."

Hickson (later): "They won't believe it. They gonna believe it one of these days. Might be too late. I knew all along they was people from other worlds up there. I knew all along. I never thought it would happen to me."

Parker: "You know yourself I don't drink."

Hickson: "I know that, son. When I get to the house I'm gonna get me another drink, make me sleep. Look, what we sittin' around for? I gotta go tell Blanche . . . what we waiting for?"

Parker (panicky): "I gotta go to the house. I'm gettin' sick. I gotta get out of here."

Hickson left his fishing companion alone. When the investigators played back the tape they heard the young man talking to himself.

Parker: "It's hard to believe . . . Oh God, it's awful . . . I know there's a God up there. . . ."

He then prayed and his words became an inaudible whisper.

Journalist Ralph Blum gives a detailed account of the Hickson–Parker case in his book *Beyond Earth: Man's Contact With UFOs.* During his own investigation of the contact report he interviewed Sheriff Diamond and asked if he believed the statements made by the two men. "First thing they wanted to do was take a lie detector test," the sheriff replied. "Charlie— he was shook bad." He added that you don't see a man of Hickson's age "break down and cry from excitement unless it's something fierce happened."

Dr. Allen Hynek, who was present during the time-regression hypnosis that both men agreed to undergo, declared later:

"There's simply no question in my mind that these men have had a very real frightening experience, the physical nature of which I am not certain about . . . They are absolutely honest. They have had a fantastic experience and also I believe it should be taken in context with experiences that others have had elsewhere in this country and in the world."

Dr. James Harder, professor of Engineering at the University of California in Berkeley and consultant to one of the largest civilian UFO organizations, the Aerial Phenomena Research Organization, supervised the regression hypnosis with a psychiatrist. His opinion was that "the experience they underwent was indeed a real one. A very strong feeling of terror is practically impossible to fake under hypnosis."

In the case of Patrolman Schirmer and Betty and Barney Hill the UFO occupants appear to have been able not only to control the minds of Earth people but also to obliterate their experiences from their conscious minds.

"We have no way of knowing how many human beings throughout the world may have been processed in this manner, since they would have absolutely no memory of undergoing the experience, and so we have no way of determining who among

The UFO Chase

One of the wildest UFO chases on record took place early in the morning of April 17, 1966. It started when Dale F. Spaur, deputy sheriff of Portage County, Ohio, stopped at a stalled car and spotted the brightly lit flying object that had been reported to his office. He was ordered to follow it. He and an assistant raced after it in their patrol car for about 70 miles, sometimes driving over 100 mph to keep it in their sight.

Forty miles east of the point at which he started, Spaur met Officer Wayne Huston of East Palestine after having talked to him by car radio. This officer saw the flying saucer too, and described it as "shaped something like an ice cream cone with a sort of partly melted top." The chase continued into neighboring Pennsylvania, ending in Conway. Officer Frank Panzanella of that town came to the scene when he saw the other policemen, and told them he had been watching the shining object of the chase for about 10 minutes. All four observers then saw the UFO rise straight up left of the moon, and disappear.

The United States Air Force Project Blue Book investigated the Spaur-UFO chase, and labeled it as a sighting of Venus. The four independent observers involved do not believe that was the right conclusion.

us has strange and sinister 'programs' lying dormant in the dark corners of his mind."

This is the view of American author John Keel, a leader among those UFO investigators who believe that flying saucers are not a physical phenomenon, and do not consist of solid matter. He thinks that UFOs have superior powers and exist alongside our world but on a totally different time scale. They are usually invisible but are capable of materializing in our world. They can take on any shape and travel at incredibly rapid speeds. Keel calls the inhabitants of the UFOs ultra-terrestrials and speculates on the reasons for their appearances to man. He suggests that perhaps the Universe is controlled and permeated by one gigantic intelligence or energy force which is all-knowing, and which is outside our concept of time and space. Throughout the Universe there are other lesser intelligences which exist at different time frequencies. The higher among these can to some extent manipulate the lower, though all are subordinate to the one main force. If this supreme intelligence wished to communicate with a fairly low form of intelligence such as man, it might choose to do so through an intermediary intelligence such as the ultraterrestrials. The information would be too complicated to be given at once, so it would be given gradually in small pieces over a long period of time. The flaw in this argument seems to be that misleading and contradictory information is often the result of exchanges between humans and ultraterrestrials. Keel has two possible explanations for this. One is that misleading information is deliberately given whenever it is felt that we are not yet ready to accept the truth. The other is that the occupants of the UFOs may be deliberately lying for some purpose of their own.

Keel believes that the ultraterrestrials are the same entities responsible for psychic phenomena and Spiritualism—another area of investigation that is full of conflict and confusion. Just as false and mischievous spirits are reported at seances, so the UFO entities appear to be deliberately trying to confuse us, says Keel. They set out to give the impression that they are from outer space to throw us off the scent, and at the same time they deliberately change their appearance and stories so that investigators will not be able to discover their true origin. The UFOs' occupants have been described variously as tall, average, and small; green, gray, and dark-skinned; of normal appearance, fishlike and monsterlike. They are said to have come from practically every planet in our solar system as well as from others in the furthest reaches of the Universe.

Either every contactee has lied about his or her experiences or else we are being visited by many different space races. Most contactees are simple, sincere people who appear to be convinced that they have had a real experience. Keel has interviewed 200 contactees who have not sought publicity about their encounters—and he has this to say about them in his book *UFOs: Operation Trojan Horse:*

"They do not write books or go on lecture tours. They show little or no interest in UFO literature. Some of them begin to experience personality deterioration after their initial contact. Others find their previously normal lives disrupted by night-

CALVIN PARKER

CHARLES HICKSON

Left: pictures from a television report on Calvin Parker and Charles Hickson, who claim to have encountered a UFO while fishing. They were taken aboard by strange faceless creatures who examined them. The man at the top is Calvin Parker; the older man below is Charles Hickson. The drawing is their version of one of the creatures. Right: Dr. James Harder and Dr. Allen Hynek as they question and interview Parker and Hickson.

Above: an artist's impression of the occupants of the UFO, based on Hickson's description. He had no memory of hair or eyes, and reported that the slitlike "mouth" didn't move.

mares and peculiar hallucinations. Poltergeists (noisy, invisible ghosts) invade their homes. Their telephones and television sets run amok. My own educated guess is that there may be 50,000 or more silent contactees in the United States alone. And new ones are being added to the list every month." Many of them may not even know they have been contacted unless, like Schirmer and the Hills, they underwent regression hypnosis to try to find out why they felt anxiety.

Since the late 19th century, when people first began reporting conversations with beings who landed in aerial craft, the witnesses have not been believed. But Keel insists that these contactees have been telling us "*what they were told* by the ufonauts," and, he insists, "*the ufonauts are the liars, not the contactees.*"

His theory began to evolve after a study of the great American UFO panic of 1896–7. The aerial craft that people reported seeing looked much like the airships then being built and designed, but not yet flown in the United States. They were often seen on the ground and their occupants, who were usually described as foreigners, appeared to be repairing them. They frequently gave accounts of where they had come from and where they were heading, together with descriptions of how their airships worked. The simple farmers who had these encounters believed they were humans with advanced airships—about which they had read much in their newspapers. But Keel's examination of these reports and an investigation of some strange side issues reveals that no one on earth could have produced the craft, nor could they have been powered in the way the occupants claimed. Moreover, if these really were visitors from space, what were they doing cruising around in crude and cumbersome airships that needed so many running repairs? Clearly they had not traveled vast distances in space in such craft. Keel decided that the ultraterrestrials were responsible, and that it was no more than an elaborate smokescreen to conceal their real purpose and identity. In the 20th century, they confused us again by taking on a modern image in line with fast-developing technology. But, says Keel, they are the same ultraterrestrials playing the same tricks and leaving us, as always, hopelessly muddled. It is a practical joke on a cosmic scale.

This fascinating hypothesis does not provide all the answers.

If ultraterrestrials are responsible, why do they need to show themselves at all? What is their mission? Conjecture along these lines could lead us into the wildest regions of science fiction, particularly as more and more cases of UFO sightings seem to contain an element of the paranormal.

Two police officers, Chief Deputy Sheriff William McCoy and Deputy Robert Goode, were driving along a highway in Brazoria County, Texas, in September 1965 discussing what to do about Goode's finger. It had been bitten by his son's pet alligator, and it was throbbing painfully. As they talked about waking a doctor at the end of their patrol, they spotted a large purple glow in the sky. It was a rectangular shaped object about 50 feet in height, and it turned and headed toward them. It was accompanied by a small blue light. Goode's window was down and he was waving his aching finger in the air. As the lights rushed toward them Goode felt a wave of heat on his hand and arm. The police officers, both frightened by the lights, accelerated and drove away. But McCoy looked back to see the UFOs rise upward, flare brilliantly, and disappear. When the two men got back to Damon, Texas, Goode realized his finger was no longer hurting him. He removed the bandage and discovered that not only was the wound no longer swollen or bleeding, but also that it was almost healed.

This cure for an alligator bite received much good-natured ridicule from the press, but healings associated with UFOs are not uncommon. Famous French researcher Aimé Michel reported the case of a doctor, who insisted on remaining anonymous. Dr. X had stepped on a mine during the Algerian War. As a result he suffered from partial paralysis of both limbs on the right side. He could no longer play the piano, at which he had been exceptionally gifted, and he walked with a pronounced limp. On a November night in 1968 he awoke at 3 a.m. to hear his young son crying. He got up to go to him. One of his legs was still swollen and painful from an accident while chopping wood three days before. After seeing to his son he noticed flashes of light outside, and on looking out saw two identical disks hovering in the sky. They had antenna from which flashes of light were being emitted at one-second intervals. As he watched the two disks merged into one and traveled toward him. A beam shone over him. He instinctively covered his eyes. There was a bang and the object dematerialized. Badly shaken, he went back to the bedroom to tell his wife about the strange object in the sky. He suddenly realized that the swelling and pain from his wood-chopping accident had vanished. Later the effects of his war wounds also disappeared. He now even plays the piano again.

Another indication of paranormal influence through apparent UFO activity came to light when a well-known Argentine attorney and his wife disappeared while driving south of Buenos Aires. Dr. Gerardo Vidal and his wife were traveling on the road from Chascomus to Maipu. When they failed to arrive at their destination friends and relatives searched the area but found no trace of them or their car. Two days later the doctor phoned from the Argentine consulate in Mexico City 4000 miles away. He reported that he had been driving from the

Whatever else may be said about the creatures who reportedly visit our Earth in their mysterious spacecraft, they are certainly varied to judge by the descriptions by the humans who encounter them. The nine pictured are a sampling of the many kinds of space people seen. Left: Baurú, Brazil on July 23, 1947. Sighted by José C. Higgins, a Brazilian survey worker. Three seven-foot-tall entities from a great disk surrounded him. They wore transparent suits inflated like rubber bags with metal boxes on their backs. They were all identical, with large round bald heads, huge round eyes, no beards, no eyebrows, and immensely long legs. Higgins, who wouldn't say if they were male or female, reported them as strangely beautiful. When they tried to capture Higgins, he eluded them by hiding.

Left: near Raveo, Italy on August 14, 1947. Sighted by Professor R. L. Johannis, writer and painter. Two dwarflike creatures appeared near a disk. They were about three feet tall, with green skin. They had great protruding eyes with vertical pupils, and yellow-green circles around their eyes instead of lids. They wore translucent blue suits with red cuffs. They interpreted one of Johannis' gestures as hostile and zapped him with some kind of ray from their belt.

Right: near High Bridge, New Jersey in June 1946. Sighted by Howard Menger, a signpainter. A beautiful woman, with long blond hair, the standard human curves, blue eyes, dressed in a semitranslucent pastel fabric. The average height of an Earth woman, and graceful. Menger had sighted her 12 years earlier when he was ten. She was friendly.

suburbs of Chascomus when a dense "fog" appeared on the road in front of them. The next thing he remembered was sitting with his wife in their parked car on an unknown road. They both had a pain at the back of the neck and the sensation of having slept for hours. Their car looked as if it had been burned by a blow torch, and they had no recollection of what had happened in the intervening 48 hours or how they had been transported from Argentina to Mexico. Time-regression hypnosis may supply the answer one day, if the Vidals agree to such a test.

More than a quarter of a century after their modern debut, flying saucers are still a mystery. More confusion and doubt exists now than when Kenneth Arnold sighted nine shining disks over Mount Rainier in 1947. But Dr. Hynek and others are sure a continued scientific study is worth the effort. There is plenty of room for new investigators willing to dedicate their time to a specialized study of the various aspects of UFO phenomena.

"Although it will be a Herculean task to cull and refine existing UFO data," Dr. Hynek writes, "I feel a rich reward awaits a person or a group that assumes this task with dedication." He considers it possible that something might be found which represents a major scientific breakthrough. "It might call for reassignment and rearrangement of many of our established concepts of the physical world, far greater even than the rearrangements that were necessary when relativity and quantum mechanics demanded entrance into our formerly cozy picture of the world."

Above: near Desert Center, California on November 20, 1952. Sighted by George Adamski, UFO researcher. Was tracking a UFO when a man appeared. About 5 feet 6 inches tall, round-faced, slightly slanted eyes and high cheekbones. Had flowing shoulder-length hair which fell in waves and was of a sandy color. Wore a one-piece garment in a dark brown, which looked much like our ski suits. Greeted Adamski cordially, and subsequently visited him as a good friend.

Above left: Caracas, Venezuela on November 28, 1954. Sighted by Gustavo Gonzales and José Ponce. Emerged from a luminous sphere. Four bristly, hairy, dwarflike creatures of amazing strength and impenetrable skin. One managed to push Gonzales 15 feet away with a single easy gesture. When Gonzales stabbed at it with his knife, the knife glanced off as if the skin were metal. All of them wore loin cloths. Their behavior was clearly hostile and aggressive. Above right: Hopkinsville, Kentucky on August 22, 1955. Sighted by the Sutton family. Apparently emerged from a spaceship seen to land in a nearby field. There were several green ghostlike figures, about three feet tall, which seemed to glow from inside. Had round heads, great elephantine ears, and a mouth slit from ear to ear. Had no visible neck and the long arms ended in claws. Stood upright, but ran on all fours. The creatures clambered all over the roof of the Sutton house, and terrorized the family throughout the night.

Above left: near Francisco de Sales, Brazil on October 15, 1957.
Sighted by Antonio Villas Boas, a farmer. Five creatures, the crew
of an egg-shaped UFO. Nearly 6 feet tall, of normal strength. Small,
light-colored eyes. Wore gray tight-fitting overalls which fastened
to a stiff helmet with three silvery tubes emerging and entering
the clothing. Had pineapple sized luminous red shield on the chest.
Examined Villas Boas, took a blood sample, and used him, he said,
for an interterrestrial breeding experiment with one of the crew.
Above right: Alto dos Cruzeiros, Brazil on October 26, 1962.
Sighted by José Camilho Filho, a mechanic. Appeared sitting on a
fallen banana tree, apparently associated with a UFO sighted nearby.
Two three-foot tall creatures with brown shrivelled skin, large
head, white hair, and large slit eyes. Wore green trousers, blue
shirts, and a luminous chest shield that flashed like a welding lamp.
Took flight and ran, colliding with each other, when they saw Filho.

**Above: Ashland, Nebraska on
December 3, 1967. Sighted by
Herbert Schirmer, a policeman.
Came out of a football shaped
UFO. Four crew members, about
five feet tall, with gray-white
skin, flat noses, and a motionless
slit mouth. Slightly slanted eyes
that did not blink, but whose pupils
widened and narrowed like a camera. Wore silvery-gray uniforms,
boots, and gloves. Winged serpent
emblem on the chest. Took Schirmer
into the spacecraft, lectured him,
and afterward induced amnesia.**

The Inhabited Universe

Man is now a space traveler. His manned landings and explorations of the moon, and the investigation of neighboring planets by space probes mark a turning point of enormous importance in Earth's development. The success of our space programs has made space flight seem as effortless as a transatlantic flight, and there are those who doubtless think that it is only lack of sufficient finance that prevents us from embarking on a full-scale investigation of the Universe.

It is not this simple. To put the whole concept of time and space into perspective, place an orange on the floor. It represents

Right: Edwin Aldrin photographed on the Moon by fellow astronaut Neil Armstrong on July 21, 1969 —man's first day on the Moon. Do today's astronauts and cosmonauts look less extraordinary than some of the reported visitors from outer space? How would an ordinary person of the last century have reacted if one of our now-familiar astronauts had appeared?

"The problem of traversing vast regions of space will... be overcome."

the Sun, the small insignificant star that is nonetheless so essential to the existence of all forms of life on our planet. The Earth, the third planet from the Sun in our solar system, would be 25 feet away and the size of a pinhead. Jupiter, the largest planet in the center of our nine-planet system, would be 130 feet away and the size of a large pea. Pluto, the outermost planet, would be a pinhead 1200 feet from the Sun. Where would the nearest star, Alpha Centaurus, be in relation to this miniature solar system? It would be approximately the distance that separates Great Britain and the United States.

Let us take an imaginary space trip setting out from the Sun—an impossibility in real terms, of course. The fastest man-made object to leave the solar system so far has been the *Pioneer 10* which, after its close approach to Jupiter in December 1973, was sped out of our planetary system at about seven miles a second.

On our imaginary trip we will travel slightly faster—at 10 miles a second or 36,000 miles per hour. At this speed it will take us six weeks to reach Mercury, the first planet in orbit around the Sun. It will take another 35 days to reach the next planet, Venus. Our own Earth is a further 30 days away. The journey on to Mars will occupy another eight weeks. As we move farther away from the center of our solar system we find the planets are spaced at greater intervals. Between Mars and the fifth planet, Jupiter, is a belt of asteroids. When our space ship passes Jupiter it will be 88 weeks after our departure. Three years will have elapsed by the time we reach the next planet, Saturn, and a further three years will have to pass before we arrive at the seventh planet, Uranus. At our speed of 10 miles a second, four more years would be required to bring us within the vicinity of Neptune. The last known planet, Pluto, would be reached 15 years after our departure. It would take us 80,000 years to reach the nearest star, and another 80,000 years if we were planning on a return journey.

With our present mode of rocket-propelled space travel, then, we are clearly confined to exploring our own solar system. The stars will have to wait. But the problems of traversing vast regions of space will undoubtedly be overcome, perhaps sooner than we expect and in ways we cannot yet imagine.

Below: this diagram shows the comparative sizes of the Sun and the planets, which are given in order of their distance from the Sun. Mercury (far left) is nearest the Sun. The others in sequence are Venus, Earth, Mars, Jupiter—the largest—Saturn, Uranus, Neptune, and Pluto, the farthest away. The broad curve at the bottom is part of the Sun.

Right: the order of the planets around the glowing Sun, with their orbits. The planets are not shown in scale. The outer planets are much further from the Sun than can be shown in a single drawing of this size. The planets, like the Moon, have no light of their own, and shine only because they reflect light from the Sun.

In the early days of UFO sightings, many believers claimed that the flying saucers were spacecraft from our neighboring planets. Mars and Venus were the main contenders as the home planets of the aliens in the sky. At that time in the late 1940s, our astronomical knowledge was not sufficient to be able to say with certainty whether life did exist on these, our closest planet neighbors. Mars appeared to have ice caps, and some astronomers had reported seeing what appeared to be artificial canals. Venus, on the other hand, was shrouded in cloud and mystery.

Even our Moon was regarded as a possible home for flying saucers—if not as the natural home of their operators, then at least as a base for visitors from farther afield.

Few UFO enthusiasts realized that those were the last years of wild conjecture about the other planets in our system. In only a few years we were walking on the surface of the Moon and landing sophisticated probes on other planets. The results of these explorations, and our continuing space program, have dashed the hopes of many UFO fans and demolished the stories of numerous contactees.

Let us embark on the imaginary space trip once more, this time stopping to examine each of the planets in the light of latest human knowledge. Our first stop is Mercury, the smallest planet, which has the distinction of also being the hottest and the coldest world in the solar system. It was formerly thought that Mercury kept the same face toward the Sun, but recent radar measurements show that it rotates on its axis once every 59 days. The surface is subjected to temperatures ranging from 752°F to −328°F and there seems to be no detectable atmosphere to moderate these extremes. In human terms it is inhospitable and unlikely to support life.

Venus viewed from the Earth is the brightest planet when it comes to within 25 million miles. It is of similar size and mass to our Earth but the similarity ends there. Its atmospheric pressure at the surface is about 90 times that of Earth, and this causes an insulating effect which maintains extremely high temperatures throughout the planet. The surface temperature remains at about 900°F day and night at the equator and at the poles. It is thought that the dense cloud layer which permanently encircles our nearest neighbor consists of a concentrated solution of sulfuric acid. Visibility at noon on the surface would be no better than at twilight on Earth, and the Venusian surroundings would be bathed in a deep red glow.

A human being would be crushed to death by the enormous pressure and fried to a crisp by the temperature in this huge planetary greenhouse. If life has developed there it will be greatly different from the forms it takes on our own planet. But there are known types of organic molecules that would be at home in the Venusian environment, so it would be foolish to dismiss the possibility of life entirely.

The next planet we explore is our own. As we approach the Earth we can see no visible signs of life, and it gives the appearance of being a cold world. The atmosphere of the globe is composed of 20 percent oxygen and 80 percent nitrogen. Space races viewing Earth from a distance may well conclude that the methane traces in the atmosphere are produced by biological processes. But for evidence of intelligent life they would need to pick up radio signals. Other civilizations may well decide that the oxygen—basically a deadly gas—would prevent life from forming. But we know that it is essential for our existence and that of many other life forms on Earth. In fact we depend on the plant life on our planet for converting carbon dioxide from the atmosphere into oxygen by photosynthesis. We also know that living organisms can survive the extreme temperatures of our planet and its different pressures. They live and thrive on the top of our highest mountains and in the depths of our deepest oceans. This adaptability of life should be kept in mind as we examine the other planets in our solar system.

The next planet on our journey is Mars, which is thought by many to be the most likely on which some form of life may have evolved. It has a very thin atmosphere and can be extremely cold,

Above: a 19th-century artist's impression of the planet Jupiter as it would look from one of its 12 satellites. The vegetation is clearly based on what grows on Earth, since little was known of the other celestial bodies. It seems to argue that other planets could support life like ours.

Below: an imaginative view of Mars by the same artist. Mars has long been the focus for most enthusiastic speculation about life elsewhere in our solar system, and the "men from Mars" have led a lively fictional existence. When the Italian astronomer Giovanni V. Schiaparelli reported canals on the surface, there were many who were convinced that there had to be intelligent life on the planet. Below right: one of the Mariner 9 photographs of the surface of Mars. Schiaparelli's canals are obviously not man-made, but the deep channels may indicate that water flowed there sometime in the past.

although the temperature can rise to as high as 77°F. It also has polar regions, but these are thought to be thin regions of frozen carbon dioxide rather than ice caps. Some astronomers regard the red planet Mars as being in the throes of an ice age. If this is so, then it is likely that when the heat of the sun turns Earth into a Venus, the same process will create an Earth out of Mars. In four billion years, if humans still exist on our planet, a mass evacuation to Mars might well take place.

One hypothesis is that Mars undergoes climatic changes each 50,000-year period. At the beginning of the cycle it has an extensive north polar region. It enjoys a period of spring and summer followed by a winter period with an extensive south polar region halfway through the cycle. Another summer period follows and then the north polar cap grows once more. During the Martian winters the dense atmosphere, according to this theory, is locked in the ice caps. In the summer they melt, forming an atmosphere that would be comfortable for us. If this is so, life on Mars may have adapted so that it hibernates during the long winter, waiting for the water that flows with the onset of summer to bring it back to life. This theory will be tested when a Viking biology experiment lands on Mars in 1976. The plan is to drop soil samples into liquid water in a search for microbes.

Our investigation of Mars has already provided a wealth of information that has changed many ideas about this fascinating planet. Mariner 9, the space probe that circled the planet in 1971, sent back over 7000 photographs. These enabled a close study of many features for the first time. We now know that there are no artificial canals on the planet; but there are deep channels which indicate that water has flowed on the surface of Mars in the past. It now seems likely that the dark areas which astronomers have seen grow and recede each year are not signs of some form of primitive vegetation, but are windblown dust stretching from impact craters.

Our journey through the solar system brings us next to Jupiter, the largest of all the planets. With a diameter of 88,700 miles, it is big enough to accommodate all the other planets in the system. It seems to be a largely gaseous body whose outer temperatures are extremely cold—in the region of −238°F. The cloud belts that encircle the planet have one particular feature, the famous Great Red Spot.

Saturn too is a giant planet that seems to be a largely gaseous body, possibly with a hard central core. It also is a cold world— at least as far as the outer regions are concerned, and these are the only ones that can be studied by our present instruments. What distinguishes it from other planets is its rings which, though only about 10 miles in thickness, extend over 170,000 miles in diameter.

The existence of Uranus was not discovered until after the invention of the telescope. It is similar to Jupiter and Saturn and its temperature is even lower at about −346°F. Neptune is much further out, and its existence was predicted before it was discovered in 1846. Astronomers had correctly deduced that deviations from the predicted orbit of Uranus were caused by another planet, and three years later they were proved right.

The existence of the last planet that is presently known in our

Recent photographs of Venus, the
brightest planet (top left), Saturn with its ever-present rings
(top right), huge Jupiter (bottom
left), and Mars (bottom right).
As more probes are launched from
the Earth to explore the far distant planets of our solar system,
the age-old speculation that life
exists outside of the Earth comes
closer to being answered. So far
the probes have disclosed many
wonders, but have not turned up
evidence of intelligent life anywhere else in the Universe.

Above: *The Man from Venus*, an illustration from a 1939 science fiction magazine. Notice how casually the Earth visitor has doffed his helmet, just as though Venus and Earth have the same kind of atmosphere. After recent Soviet instrument landings on Venus, our ideas about that planet are changing rapidly. However, conclusions are still a matter of scientific debate and controversy.

Above left: *Life on Titan*, a 1940 science fiction illustration. Titan, one of the larger of Jupiter's satellites, is now known as Callisto. Its density is so low that scientists think it may be composed of ice—even monsters would hardly find life sustainable in those conditions.

solar system, Pluto, was also predicted when it was discovered that both the orbits of Uranus and Neptune were still being deflected from their orbits by another body. Percival Lowell made the forecast in 1914 but failed to find it. It was not until 1930, some years after his death, that it was discovered. A mystery remains, however, for the planet seems too small to account for the effects produced in the orbits of the other two planets. The possibility exists that a tenth planet, so far undetected, circles the Sun.

Pluto is a small frozen body which takes 248 years to make a single orbit of the Sun. Its orbit is so eccentric, however, that at times it comes closer to the Sun than Neptune.

During our space voyage we will have encountered a belt of large lumps of rock orbiting in the enormous gap of 350 million miles which separates Mars and Jupiter. These are the minor planets or asteroids. There is a mystery about their origin. Some astronomers believe that they are the material out of which all planets are formed. There are others, however, who regard the asteroid belt as the remnants of a planet. Perhaps it was like Earth and developed a civilization with technical skills, which subsequently resulted in not only the annihilation of the people but also the disintegration of the planet into 40,000 pieces.

Not only has our journey through our solar system failed to find other intelligent life forms, but the evidence also shows that life would develop in different ways on our neighboring planets because of the different temperatures and pressures. So the stories of humanlike space people in flying saucers from Mars, Venus, Saturn, and elsewhere are clearly fiction. But what are the prospects of advanced civilizations existing elsewhere in the Universe?

Various astronomers and space scientists have turned their attention to this question with different results. But none has said life cannot exist. After all, we know so little about the Universe that we cannot speak with certainty on such matters. Logic, however, tells us that if life has evolved on one planet orbiting an ordinary star, then the chances are that the same or a similar evolutionary process has occurred elsewhere. Since this must have occurred in many cases long before the Earth was created, the chances are that there are numerous civilizations with abilities so great that they are beyond our comprehension. Our own technology has made astonishing leaps forward in the 20th century, and it is impossible for anyone to predict with certainty what developments, discoveries, and achievements will be made in the next hundred years.

It was only at the beginning of this century that man made his first flight in a powered craft. That distinction goes to Wilbur and Orville Wright who, on December 17, 1903, managed to make a number of flights. The longest covered a distance of 852 feet and lasted 59 seconds. In a little over 50 years, the transportation of large numbers of people through the air became commonplace, and we had designed and launched the first artificial satellite to orbit our planet—Sputnik 1 on October 4, 1957. Progress in space flight has been even more rapid. Twelve years after the Soviet Union spacecraft escaped Earth's gravitational pull, two Americans landed on the surface of the Moon. Neil Armstrong became the first human to step onto another body in space. The footprints that he and his fellow astronaut Edwin Aldrin left behind will last a million years. That turning point in the history of Earth took place on July 21, 1969.

Three years later the United States launched the space probe Pioneer 10 on a trajectory that took it across the orbit of Mars and safely through the asteroid belt in about seven months, and on to Jupiter. The gravitational pull of that planet caused Pioneer 10 to change its course, and it flew past the orbit of Uranus and out into space. It will continue to travel for two million years before approaching the star Aldebaran, and ten billion years before entering the planetary system of another star.

On board Pioneer 10 is a gold-anodized aluminum plaque etched with a message from Earth. It shows our solar system in a coded form with clues which, though they would mystify most Earth people, are designed to tell a superior race exactly where the spacecraft originated. The plaque includes line drawings of a naked man and woman. (It says something about the Earth's development that some newspapers felt it necessary to censor the drawings—removing the woman's nipples and the man's sexual organs. Some newspapers that published the uncensored sketch received letters from irate readers accusing the space agency of spreading filth throughout the Universe.)

The man who conceived the message from Earth is Dr. Carl Sagan, Professor of Astronomy and Space Sciences at Cornell University. His artist wife, Linda, drew the terrestrials on the golden greeting card. Dr. Sagan, one of exobiology's most articulate spokesmen, has described sending a message in this form as "very much like a shipwrecked sailor casting a bottled message into the ocean—but the ocean of space is much vaster than any ocean on Earth." The chances of an extraterrestrial race finding the silent Pioneer and its coded message depends both on such a civilization having an extensive capability for interstellar space flight, and being able to intercept and recover such space derelicts before they enter the gravitational pull of a planet or star and are burned up. Messages in bottles have been washed ashore in time to save a shipwrecked mariner, but it is rare. The chances are that Pioneer 10 will disappear into space and not be intercepted until long after the Earth and all its inhabitants have expired. But there are far better ways of attempting to make contact with other worlds, and of trying to detect if they are attempting to communicate with us.

Radio waves were discovered coming from the center of our galaxy in 1931, though it was not until about 20 years later that the science of radio astronomy emerged as being of great importance. Optical telescopes, in use before radio waves, have obvious drawbacks. They can be used only in areas where the weather permits long periods of observation. Even then, they peer at the teeming world of space through our atmosphere, and that inevitably hinders clear observation. A radio telescope collects signals from space, magnifying them and converting them into detectable signals. It can operate in weather conditions not conducive to optical viewing. Radio waves are simply a form of electromagnetic radiation, like light.

"There appears to be a fair chance that advanced extraterrestrial civilizations are sending radio signals our way, and that we have the technology to receive such signals," says Dr. Sagan.

Project Ozma was the first attempt to listen to broadcasts from extraterrestrial societies. It was organized in 1960 by Frank Drake at the National Radio Astronomy Observatory. Two stars were studied at one radio frequency for two weeks. The results, not surprisingly, were negative. The Soviet Union has a more ambitious project and further studies by the United States will give the experimenters a greater chance of success. "All in all," says Dr. Sagan, "perhaps a few hundred nearby stars will be examined at one or two frequencies. But even the most optimistic calculations on the distances to the nearest stars suggest that hundreds of thousands to millions of stars must be

Above: the Wright brothers make the first flight in history on December 17, 1903 in Kittyhawk, N.C. None of their trials that day lasted a full minute. But the Air Age that the Wrights opened advanced with electrifying speed, and it was only 54 years later that mankind reached outer space.

Below: Sputnik I, the world's first artificial satellite, launched by the Soviets on October 4, 1957. It weighed 184 pounds, and its name is translated as "fellow wayfarer."

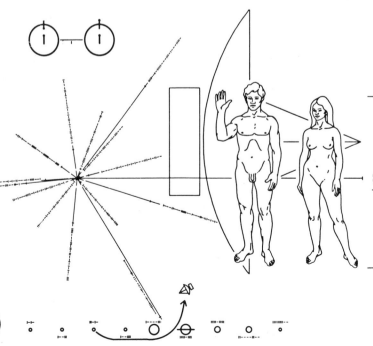

Above: the Apollo II lunar module rises from the surface of the Moon to meet the command module for the flight back to Earth on July 21, 1969. Astronauts had finally walked on the Moon, and stood on the threshold of space.

Left: the drawing that appeared on the anodized gold plaque put aboard Pioneer 10, the first spacecraft launched to travel beyond our solar system. The coded message looks obscure. But it is hoped it would be intelligible to any beings who are sufficiently advanced scientifically to be able to intercept and recover Pioneer 10 from limitless space.

examined before an intelligible signal from one of them will be received."

For the first time, says Dr. Sagan, we have the tools to make contact with civilizations on planets of other stars. "It is an astonishing fact," he writes in his book *The Cosmic Connection: An Extraterrestrial Perspective*, "that the great 1000-foot-diameter radio telescope of the National Astronomy and Ionosphere Center, run by Cornell University in Arecibo, Puerto Rico, would be able to communicate with an identical copy of itself anywhere in the Milky Way Galaxy."

We have the expertise, but do we have the time? Radio waves, like light waves, travel at the astonishing speed of 186,000 miles a second. Because of the vast distances in space, it is easier to talk in terms of light years rather than Earth miles. A radio wave from our planet will travel 6000 billion miles in one year. While teams of Earth scientists have been listening to radio signals from space in the hope of receiving messages from other intelligent beings, others have been working on transmitting radio signals. After all, if everyone listened and no one transmitted, every populated planet would conclude that they were alone in the Universe. So in 1974 a three-minute coded signal was beamed out from the huge Arecibo radio telescope. It was aimed at the star cluster Messier 13 on the edge of the Milky Way, and it will take 24,000 years to reach its destination. The double-frequency message gives scientific information about life on Earth and its technical advancement. But by the time it reaches the 300,000 stars in the Messier 13 cluster it will be out of date. It is likely that a planet orbiting one of those stars will also be searching the heavens for signs of life. If it responds to the Earth signal it will take another 24,000 years for the reply to be received. As Dr. Drake, the Arecibo center's director, observes, "None of us here will ever know if it worked."

A meaningful dialogue, therefore, seems out of the question. Even if we pick up intelligent signals that tell us something about the beings transmitting them, they will have evolved well beyond that stage, or possibly even have perished, by the time their message arrives. The problem of time lapse is present in every field of astronomy. When we look at the nearest star we see it as it was four years ago. But some stars appear to us now as they were in biblical times or before. It is possible that they have grown brighter or duller, exploded, or changed in other ways, but we have no way of knowing it until many years after the event.

These limitations are imposed on us so long as we remain stationary observers. Einstein's theory of relativity has shown that space travel, even over vast distances, could be a reality in a few years because of an effect known as time dilation. If we were able to travel close to the speed of light, time as measured by our watches or heartbeats would pass far more slowly than on Earth.

Our Sun is part of a two hundred billion star complex that forms the Milky Way Galaxy—just one of billions of galaxies in the Universe. We are located near the edge of our spiral galaxy, and light from its center takes 30,000 years to reach us. At the velocity of light it would take an Earth spaceship over 60,000

Above: the world's largest and most sensitive radio telescope at the National Astronomy and Ionosphere Center, run by Cornell University in Arecibo, Puerto Rico. The 600-ton triangular platform of the telescope hovers over its 1000-foot diameter reflector bowl. In November 1974 it beamed out a radio message giving coded information about the Earth and its technical achievements. It was aimed at a star cluster on the edge of our Milky Way galaxy.

Above: Dr. Frank Drake, the director of the Arecibo center. He initiated Project Ozma, the attempt to communicate with other intelligent life in space. Two stars were studied intensively for two full weeks. Below: the 140-foot diameter radio telescope at the National Radio Astronomy Observatory, located in Greenbank, West Virginia. Dr. Drake used it on Project Ozma to listen for messages.

years to cross from one end of the galaxy to the other, yet those on board would be able to complete the trip in less than a lifetime. "With the appropriate vehicle," says Dr. Sagan, "we could circumnavigate the Galaxy and return almost 200,000 years later, as measured on Earth. Naturally, our friends and relatives would have changed some in the interval—as would our society and probably even our planet." Indeed, according to special relativity, it is even possible to circumnavigate the entire Universe in a lifetime, returning to our planet many billions of years in our future.

As long as we can develop a means of traveling close to the speed of light, it seems, there should be no difficulty in exploring billions of worlds. The problem is that we would never be able

Above: Dr. Carl Sagan, director of planetary studies at Cornell University, New York. He is one of the foremost spokesmen of exobiology—a new field of study that deals with the possibility of extraterrestrial life and the means for detecting it.

Opposite: the Pleiades, or Seven Sisters, in the constellation of Taurus, 490 million light years away from the Earth. Is there a hospitable world like our own circling around one of these stars? Could it send visitors to our planet? Will we ever know if in fact it has already done so?

to report back in a meaningful way. But perhaps the Universe has an answer to that problem as well.

The stars are, in simple terms, controlled hydrogen bombs. The source of their energy is nuclear fusion. It is thought that stars were formed out of hydrogen and helium, which contracted and compacted causing violent collisions of atoms at the center. After a complex chain reaction, stars were formed, often throwing off their outer skins or even exploding and causing new stars to be born. Smaller condensations near these stars were not large enough to produce nuclear reactions and become stars. Instead they became planets.

It is the death of stars that is causing the most exciting conjecture among astronomical theorists. A star over $2\frac{1}{2}$ times as massive as our Sun is thought to collapse at the end of its life with such force that it cannot be stopped. It contracts to one mile across and shrinks further, crushing its matter until its density passes that of the nucleus of an atom. As this collapse continues the gravitational field in its vicinity increases to such an extent that matter cannot leave the star, and light is trapped. A *photon* (particle of light) traveling at the speed of light will follow a curved path and fall back into the star. As a result the dying star is dark. It exerts a powerful gravitational pull, but cannot be seen. Such stars are known as "black holes." Though at the present this is still a theoretical concept, black holes almost certainly exist. Cygnus X–1 shows all the signs of being a *binary* star—that is, a pair of stars revolving around each other— except that only one star is visible. Yet the one that is invisible should be 10 times the mass of the Sun and extremely bright. Therefore it is probably a black hole.

Dr. Sagan, like many other astronomers, believes that theoretically there could be a million other stars with planets, in our own galaxy alone, which have advanced civilizations at this moment. If that is so, some of them, using black holes to speed their travel across the universe, may be visiting Earth—though why they should show special interest in a planet at such an early stage of development is difficult to understand. It could explain the reported speed of UFOs and their sudden disappearances. Perhaps we are wasting our time with radio messages. It may be like banging drums to send our communications from one place to another, unaware that all around us in the air are unseen messages and radio and TV signals. Without the right receivers, they remain invisible and inaudible. Perhaps our visitors are just as intangible.

Unidentified flying objects may even be piloted by a former race of Earth people who, having explored the Universe, have returned to find their civilization destroyed and a new, younger civilization in its place. The coming of the flying saucers may prove to have nothing to do with space visitors when the mystery is eventually solved. But the worldwide interest has heralded the space age and prepared us for an encounter with other civilizations.

We are certainly not alone in the Universe. And even if every flying saucer so far can be proved to be no more than misidentification, hallucination, or deliberate fabrication, the next one may be for real.

Picture Credits